To

David.

Happy Birthday 1993.

Love
Uncle Noel + Auntie Jean.

CARLING'S
ENGLAND

CARLING'S ENGLAND

The Making of the
World Cup Team

BARRY NEWCOMBE

HARVILL
An Imprint of HarperCollins*Publishers*

First published in Great Britain in 1991
by Harvill, an imprint of HarperCollinsPublishers
77/85 Fulham Palace Road,
Hammersmith, London W6 8JB

9 8 7 6 5 4 3 2 1

BRITISH LIBRARY CATALOGUING IN PUBLICATION DATA

A catalogue record for this book
is available from the British Library

ISBN 0-00-272130-9

Typeset in Plantin Light by Butler & Tanner Ltd, Frome and London

Printed and bound in Great Britain by
Butler & Tanner Ltd, Frome and London

For Maureen, Kerry and Andrew,
and all The Saints who put me on the road.

CHAPTER 1

Those close to Nigel Melville on that March afternoon at Twickenham knew at once that something was terribly wrong. It was the 44th minute of England's match against Ireland in the five nations' championship of 1988, and Melville had taken what felt to him like the whole force of the Irish pack after he had passed a ball inside the shadow of the West stand.

The players were sickened by what they saw. Melville's right foot had turned 180 degrees. Apart from that obvious dislocation it would soon be discovered that Melville had broken his leg as well, and as he disappeared into the tunnel on his way to the dressing room and then to hospital, everyone in the England camp knew it was the end of the road, in international terms, for Melville. He was 27.

Melville's time at the top of international rugby had been bedevilled by injury. He had always been a player of distinction, making his mark at Aireborough Grammar School in Yorkshire before going on to captain England Schools in 1979, first for their matches against the home countries and France, then on a tour to Australia and New Zealand.

He continued to be regarded as captaincy material whenever he played, but frequent absences because of injury prevented his progress being as spectacular as at one time seemed possible. He had one of the quickest pairs of hands ever witnessed in an England scrum-half and his abilities were utilized by the British Lions even ahead of his own country. In 1983, several months before winning his national colours, he was asked to join the Lions tour of New Zealand as a replacement. He was injured there as well.

In the autumn of 1984 Melville was chosen to play for England for the first time. Unusually he was simultaneously appointed captain, but his leadership became a stop-start affair, mirroring his career. He played four matches in 1985, none of them as captain, led England in the championship of 1986, then after a year off because of injuries, came back in 1988.

The Ireland match which ended Melville's career was his 13th for England and his seventh as captain. It was the final game in the championship that year and England, who had won only once, were searching for a victory to end the season on a respectable note, if nothing else. When Melville departed, England were 0–3 behind due to a dropped goal from Michael Kiernan who had obtained the ball, ironically, after Melville had been dispossessed just four minutes earlier.

Melville had not even left the pitch before England adjusted their team. Richard Harding of Bristol, the replacement scrum-half, saw what had happened, tore off his tracksuit and ran on. The captaincy was taken over by John Orwin, a Yorkshireman like Melville, who was leading the pack from the second row. At the same time Clive Norling, the Welsh referee, blew for the end of the first half.

What happened next will for ever remain part of English rugby folklore. In his half-time talk Orwin seized on the emotion created by Melville's absence, reminded the players that what they did next they did for the departed captain, and asked them to win the match. Harding had been sitting in the stands, and said that from his vantage point it was obvious that England had only to start spreading the ball wide to turn the game.

The punishment of the Irish began within a matter of

seconds of the restart. From the first scrum of the second half, Harding called for an attack. The ball was won and worked quickly to Rory Underwood on the right wing. With time and space Underwood surged into his sprint and avoided three attempts to tackle him before being halted close to the Irish line, where his flanker Gary Rees appeared in support and scored.

This did two things. For Underwood, who had won 21 caps on the left wing but was playing only his second match on the right, came confirmation that he was equally effective on either flank. For England came the realization that they had both the players and the pace to turn the game upside-down.

Five more tries followed and England won the game 35–3, their largest winning margin over Ireland. In a heady second-half, England scored with astonishing regularity, with Underwood claiming the last two tries. The match also launched a less familiar face on to the England scene – Chris Oti, who was playing his first game at Twickenham on the wing, scored a hat trick of tries in a period of eleven minutes. The crowd bubbled and roared and exploded, clearly feeling that a new dawn was upon English rugby.

There was one extra fixture that season, also against Ireland, a game to celebrate the Dublin Millenium. Oti, injured, did not play and neither did the No. 8, Dean Richards, who was suspended for a game as punishment for damaging the Calcutta Cup. Two weeks before the England–Ireland match Richards and John Jeffrey, the Scottish forward, had taken the famous silver cup onto the streets of Edinburgh following the after-match dinner. High jinks it may have seemed at the time, but the Cup was damaged and misshapen, and cost several thousand pounds to repair. Richards escaped with a lesser degree of punishment than Jeffrey because he missed only the Dublin match, while Jeffrey had to forgo a close season tour to Zimbabwe. The Scotland–England game which preceded the cup damage was the last in the championship for Scotland.

England, under Orwin's captaincy, went to Dublin buoyant and confident. They won the game 21–10 and, soon after that, a tour party to go to Australia was chosen. Orwin, who had been captain for one and a half matches, was made tour captain as well. Considering all the other candidates Orwin was more than fortunate to win the vote from the England management. Players with the potential leadership qualities of Brian Moore, Rob Andrew and Richard Harding were passed over. It was a hasty decision, but it was easy to understand the reasons for it. It was greatly to influence what happened subsequently with the England captaincy.

The tour to Australia was not a success. It came only a year after the first World Cup, when England had been based in Sydney and had lost to Australia in the first match of the competition, 6–19. Again England could make no impression on Australia, losing both Tests. On the other side of the Tasman Sea, Wales had been losing even more spectacularly to New Zealand, who created such havoc in Welsh thinking that it was clear the Welsh would take some years to recover.

England too had to make major changes. They were due to play Australia again in the autumn of 1988, and it was clear that Orwin would not continue in the side, either as captain or player. Thus England not only had to reconstruct the side; they had to find a new captain.

A few weeks before the autumn match against Australia the telephone rang in the south-west London home of Bill and Pam Carling, parents of Will Carling, a centre three-quarter who had made his first appearance for England at the start of 1988. The caller was Geoff Cooke and he left a message asking Carling to ring him.

Cooke, who was at the end of his first year as England manager, had always assumed that Nigel Melville would be a long-term captain from the spring of 1988 onwards. With Melville gone, Orwin discarded, and a need for continuity to be established, Cooke decided that the next captain would be appointed for at least a season.

Carling had given up a planned career in the Army so that he could devote more time to rugby, and as he threaded his way home that evening from his new job as a trainee executive with Mobil, he gave no thought to the forthcoming England selection. He was young, he was good, he was fit, and he had no reason to expect anything other than to remain in the team.

The message to ring Cooke brought the first stirrings of doubt into Carling's mind. He knew the set-up well enough. If you were a new boy in the England team, the welcome came from the coach, Roger Uttley. A conversation with Cooke was distinctly different. Invariably it meant that you were out, with an accompanying explanation of the reasons.

Carling could not believe that he had been dropped. He went through his year, from the excitement of winning his first cap against France in Paris, then on through all the other bits and pieces of his five matches with England, and could not think what he had done wrong. With his brother, Marcus, and his mother in the house, he picked up the telephone in their kitchen and dialled Geoff Cooke's number in Yorkshire.

When Carling's call came in, Cooke talked in general terms for a while before asking Carling if he would like to captain the side. There followed a stunned silence, as if Carling had gone off the line. Then came his astonished acceptance. The first bonding between manager and captain was achieved courtesy of British Telecom.

As Carling talked he scribbled on a piece of paper and pushed it towards his brother – "I am the captain", it read. Marcus shouted the news to his mother and the excitement rose in the house. Carling completed the call, remembering that Cooke had asked him to keep the news quiet until the official announcement two days later. Marcus looked at him. "You lucky bugger," he said.

The next day, Carling was a spectator at a match in London. In the bar afterwards the subject of the England team was much discussed and everybody made their choices and gave their reasons. It was typical rugby club bar talk and all sorts of names were put forward. Several people were suggested as likely captains – none of them Carling.

Aware of the official announcement due the next morning and the need to be sharp for a training session, Carling decided to leave. As his parting shot he told his companions: "I can tell you who is going to be England captain," he said. "It's me."

The assembly broke into laughter and no one thought any more of it. The next day Geoff Cooke told the world and the era of William David Charles Carling as captain of the England rugby team had begun.

CHAPTER 2

Why Carling? At the age of 22 he was the youngest player for 57 years to be asked to captain England. In the team which England chose to play with him he was also the youngest player. The three new caps nominated in the team, Andy Harriman, a wing from Harlequins, Dewi Morris, a scrum-half then playing with Liverpool St Helen's and Paul Ackford, a lock from Harlequins, were aged 24, 24 and 30, respectively.

The same arguments which had applied to last summer's tour captaincy of Australia – that Rob Andrew and Brian Moore were among the chief candidates – should have applied again. Both had moved into a position of seniority in the England squad. Andrew as a maturing decision maker at fly-half and Moore as the most vociferous of the forwards who always had something to say on everything.

However, when Cooke announced Carling as captain he had another surprise. Carling was not captain just for the match against Australia. The plan was for Carling to remain captain over the three-year period which stretched almost exactly from the England–Australia match to the final of the 1991 World Cup, also at Twickenham. Cooke explained: "We have had a succession of short-term captaincies and the feeling was that we had to establish an England captain who, though it is early for him, would take us through the next three seasons and into the 1991 World Cup."

Cooke was a long-term appointment as well. His decision meant that England's leadership for the World Cup was locked in with Cooke as manager, Carling as captain, Roger Uttley as coach and John Elliott, a hooker from Nottingham who had been a selector under the previous England management headed by Mike Weston, continuing in that role.

Dependent on form and fitness, factors which Carling fully understood and agreed with, the No.13 shirt and the captaincy would be his all the way to the World Cup – and presumably beyond, if future management retained belief in him.

Andrew was discussed as a possible captain and very few would have argued against him; but it was felt that he was under pressure in his pivotal role at fly-half and that he needed the captaincy, in Cooke's words, "like a hole in the head".

So Andrew dropped out of the reckoning. It was soon clear that Carling was the only viable alternative. Cooke felt that Carling was already a world-class centre, that he was likely to hold a place in the England side for some years – and that he would become a good captain. Cooke noted Carling's strong character, a degree of sensitivity which he hid quite well, and a combination of arrogance and selfishness which Cooke considered essential to a top sportsman. Cooke also felt that Carling's method of dealing with people enabled his enthusiasm to transmit itself to others. Cooke had seen many of the same qualities in Melville. He had also been watching Carling since he was in the Yorkshire Schools side.

No other country in contention for the next World Cup had felt the need to appoint a captain as early as England had done. Equally, most of these countries knew, as England knew, that whoever had led them in the 1987 World Cup would not be leading them in 1991. England's declaration of their hand was a sign of immense confidence in Carling and a complete gamble as well. Nobody could have predicted how he would react or how the players would react to him.

Carling did not exactly have a lengthy track record of captaincy. He led the England Schools side in the second of the two seasons he played in that team. He had been captain of various school teams on an occasional basis and at Sedbergh, his final school before he went to Durham University, Carling had captained the senior team twice in less important Easter term matches – just twice, and they were two defeats.

However, he made a point of listening closely to all the captains he played with and he read, too, the solid comments contained in the captain's book at Sedbergh. This book is the property of the rugby captain of the day and is a record of reactions to the way the Sedbergh team performs and action taken by the captain as a result. He was also greatly impressed by the New Zealander, Graham Mourie, who captained the All Blacks when Carling was in his early teens. He watched Mourie as often as he could on television, listening to what he said about leadership and noting how Mourie always seemed to have an edge of fitness in the late stages of important matches. And if ever Carling wanted some inspiration he could always go back to the example set by Andrew Harle from Durham, who had led the side at Sedbergh and had impressed Carling no end with his ability to command the team's attention and to encourage them to focus on their objectives.

None of this could help Carling now. He was out on his own, thrust into a job which paid nothing yet which demanded a great deal in terms of character, example, commitment, fitness, durability, "sufferability" and diplomacy. He had to be one of his team but aloof from them at the same time. He had to criticize as much as he would cajole. He had to play one of the fastest and most physical team games at pace and think beyond himself at the same time as he was creating. Almost everything he did off the pitch would be observed by someone, and if the pressures affected him and he was brusque or rude or snappy he would be criticized.

For a time Carling's own game would suffer as he went

through his first season as captain of England with the twin pressures of being leader for the first time and carrying a nagging shin injury which meant each game was an agony of resolution. On the field he was coach to the team, because that was the nature of things, but nobody was coaching him any more. Yet he was still a young man, with much to learn.

Apart from all the duties of player management and contact, he had to act as link between his players and the England management and to be in contact with the hierarchy of the Rugby Football Union, the governing body of English rugby. He had to get to know and then develop an understanding with the people who administered the game. Sometimes this came easily to him, sometimes not. He had to create a circle of people whom he could trust and whom he could use as a sounding board for his ideas. He became an integral part of the England selection process, given powers of advice which no other captain had enjoyed.

As he had risen in stature in the game he had established a relationship with those who write and broadcast on rugby, but from the day of his appointment everything he said carried a different emphasis. He was speaking for England and about England, and what he said helped to portray the image of England to the world at large. He had to think on his feet within seconds of completing a game and answer series of questions when his body was aching and his mind was either racing through the stratosphere in the moment of victory or plunging terrible depths because a match had been lost.

No international side is watched and reported on, at home or abroad, at the same level as England. Carling could never have been aware of this continuing responsibility when he accepted the captaincy; but his eagerness to handle it was obvious.

Because Carling was young, articulate and opinionated, interest in him was not confined to his rugby. He moved from the sports pages and programmes to magazines and the women's pages – although some of the more detailed examinations afforded leaders of sport in Britain did not affect him, since he provided no evidence of a controversial nature.

He became a television personality. At first he was talking to this camera and that camera about England's playing methods and their hopes and ambitions. Then he appeared in videos on English rugby which were an in-house production. England's dressing room and team talks and match preparation, once sacrosanct, became available to the public at large and showed there was not much mystique about it anyway.

Carling would commentate on matches when he had the opportunity. He would be invited to appear on shows such as "Wogan" and air his views to an audience which might not necessarily know about rugby football, yet saw it represented through him.

When first chosen by England in 1988, Carling was described, incorrectly, as a "yuppie". Later he might have had the attributes of a young upwardly mobile person of the eighties. He was careful about his suits, his shoes and general appearance.

Quite rapidly Carling became a higher-profile England captain than any of his predecessors. This was partially of his own seeking, partially because of the demands of an ever-widening interest in rugby and mostly because the Rugby Football Union was promoting the game as never before.

At one end of the scale he was the captain of the England team, responsible initially for the team he took with him into matches, for the squad at large, and then responsible to the Rugby Football Union in other aspects of leadership which included speaking at after-match dinners. Then there was the public relations angle, which was not just the 96 hours or so which comprise the build-up and wind-down period to the playing of an international match but all the other calls and queries which come in at unexpected times and places. Finally, there was the responsibility to the game itself, to every single club and each one of its players from Berwickupon-Tweed in the north all the way to St Just in Cornwall in the west.

Everywhere that Carling turned he trod new ground, simply because no one had ever been appointed as captain for such a long period before and because there was always the beckoning target of the World Cup. On his appointment that target stood three years away; that time would pass in the blink of an eye.

Meanwhile Nigel Melville underwent four operations and waited two years before he dared play rugby again. He returned as a full back in a rugby festival in Brussels and gradually built himself to a level where he could play again for his local club at Otley in Yorkshire. He picked up the threads with Otley so successfully that he became a regular member of their first team and played a full part in the club's promotion to Division Three of the Courage Clubs Championship in the 1990–1 season. In international terms, however, both he and the selectors knew that his time was over, even though he was still a relatively young man. For him it was all a question of what might have been.

CHAPTER 3

Carling was born in the early hours of 12 December 1965, at the maternity hospital in Bradford-on-Avon. He weighed 7lb. 15oz., was 20 inches long and had a head circumference of $13\frac{3}{4}$ inches. Eighteen months earlier his brother, Marcus, had been born in the same bed, and at that time young Will was expected to follow both father and brother into the Army.

The Carling births took place in Wiltshire because their father, Bill, a lieutenant-colonel in the Air Corps, was stationed at Warminster. A helicopter pilot, Carling senior served in the Army from 1960 for twenty-five years, leaving in 1985 to take up a new career in the City of London. Bill Carling's rugby football interests reflected the movements in his career because he played prop forward for Cardiff, Bath, Blackheath, Cornwall, and at other times in Hong Kong and elsewhere in the Far East. Carling senior did not have a major influence on his son's playing technique for the simple reason that he was in the front row and therefore had fewer opportunities than at centre, where Will was so spectacular. However, his good track record and his understanding of the way rugby men thought and felt enabled him to advise Will when called upon to do so.

Pam Carling knew what she was in for when she married her husband and was determined that her two sons would regard wherever they lived as home. So Marcus and Will became used to the various parts of the household and their own toys moving around with them wherever their father was posted.

Inevitably the style of army life and its phraseology made an impact on both Carling sons. In his first days as England captain Will Carling often seemed to be describing an army platoon and applying the ideals of leadership which had been around him in his boyhood. However, it is a fallacy to suggest that Carling was using the style of the Special Air Service in his approach to the England captaincy. While it is true that he would have met retired officers of the SAS in his youth and maybe some of their jargon rubbed off on him, he had no contact at all with serving men of the SAS.

The baby Carling might not have been impressed with what he saw had he been able to examine the state of English rugby at the time of his birth. In the 1965 championship, England finished fourth with one win, a draw and two defeats. No one knew then that the defeat to Wales in Cardiff that year would start the depressingly long series of un-rewarded visits to the Arms Park by England.

Law changes in 1965 were designed to create more space for the backs. From set pieces a ten-yard line was established with the aim of reducing the effect of the defence and giving the attacking side more room.

Despite this, England scored two tries only in their four games and their win, over France, depended much on the huge kicking of Mike Weston who had been a centre of distinction but was playing his first game for England at fly-half.

Weston first played for England in 1960, and in 1962 played all four Tests for the British Lions on their tour of South Africa. A naturally gifted ball-player, with the hard steel of Durham in his make-up, he could kick the ball higher and harder than most of his contemporaries or successors.

He plugged away with his kicking to maintain the pressure on France and tried the same again in the match with Scotland – in which the Scots led by 3–0 going into injury time. England were saved from defeat by a remarkable run from a little-known wing, Andy Hancock, winning only the second of his three English caps. England held a Scottish attack in their own half, re-won the ball, and Weston passed to Hancock outside him. The stocky wing set off on a run up the west side which spanned some 90 yards and put him on a path around the Scottish back-row forwards. He survived a tackle attempt by the full back, Stewart Wilson, and kept ahead of a despairing chase by Iain Laughland. Nobody had seen a try like that before by an Englishman at Twickenham, and although the conversion attempt was wide, England were at least saved from defeat.

Weston's span as a key figure in English rugby was to stretch on until Carling was almost 22. He moved from player to selector, and when the first World Cup was announced, England appointed him as team manager, the first to be so titled. He approached his new job with a thoroughness which characterized all his positions in rugby football.

When England made their first tour overseas in 1963, to New Zealand and Australia, Weston was their captain. It was a mission that would be considered crazy these days because England took on a programme of six games in 17 days. They played New Zealand on successive Saturdays and Australia only three days after the second Test against the All Blacks.

It was a daunting programme for a country and a team totally unused to the demands of touring. Here were the 1963 champions of the Northern Hemisphere, the first home Union to visit New Zealand, trying to take the All Blacks without three of their first-choice backs. New Zealand won the first Test 21–11. The second was a much closer contest, which the All Blacks took 9–6 in a match characterized by a brave performance from Mike Davis, a young lock from Torquay winning his fifth cap, who dislocated a shoulder in the first half but played on.

Against Australia, in soggy conditions, England were outscored by four tries to three and lost 9–18. Australia thus established an ascendancy over England which was to continue through the years whenever England visited Australia.

England's tour to New Zealand and Australia was the only one to encompass both countries. They were not the first of those involved in the five nations' championship to play outside Europe, because Scotland, in 1960, and Ireland, in 1961, had both toured South Africa. Wales also went to South Africa in 1964, losing the only Test 3–24 in Durban and returning home to sow the seeds of a coaching revolution which was not only to affect the Welsh game but that of England, their major rival, as well.

By 1965 England had been playing international rugby for 94 years. Their first game was against Scotland in 1871, at Raeburn Place in Edinburgh. England travelled north in third-class railway carriages, with bare boards, and played 20-a-side with two periods of 55 minutes each. The average weight of the England players was 12st. 3lb., and this first venture on to the international field ended in defeat. Scotland won by two tries to one.

Since then, England have won the Grand Slam nine times – although only three times since 1928 – and are the only one of the home countries to have beaten New Zealand, South Africa and Australia. Yet it could be said that throughout their international history England have remained unfulfilled. In the five nations' championship England won 52.5 per cent of their matches in the 1950s. This dropped to 37.5 per cent in the 1960s and a grating 26.8 per cent in the 1970s, when they were outscored by 91 tries to 44.

Frustration grew. Demands for England to have a proper coach were not answered until 1969. Different in-depth studies of the game in England did not answer the calls for a new competitive structure such as those which existed in the Southern Hemisphere. Then in 1972 came the first breakthrough with the introduction of a national cup competition. Even so, 15 more years passed before clubs in England at last formed themselves into a league.

None of this left England ready for the challenge of the World Cup in 1987, as their heritage suggested they should have been. They did not initially share the enthusiasm of other nations for the World Cup when it was first announced and the venue confirmed as Australia and New Zealand. For a nation with one of the largest playing populations, they did not acquit themselves well. At least the World Cup proved that there could be no going back to the cosier days when life for an international player meant four matches in the five nations' championship, an occasional game against a touring team from Australia, New Zealand or South Africa and not much else.

However, in the years before 1965 there were more than enough heroes within the English game and two particularly special captains – Wavell Wakefield and Eric Evans. Both made an indelible mark on the rugby of their country.

CHAPTER 4

William Wavell Wakefield was born in 1898 and when he died, as the first Lord Wakefield of Kendal, in the summer of 1983, he was buried from the chapel at Sedbergh School. Carling, as one of Sedbergh's better-known old boys, was fully aware of the deep attachment which Wakefield had to the school throughout his life.

Wakefield did not confine his energies to rugby. He was an outstanding athlete whose sporting interests encompassed athletics, cricket, skiing and scuba diving. He was elected a Member of Parliament in 1935 but throughout a wide-ranging career in politics and business he never lost contact with rugby, his first love. He first played for Sedbergh at the age of 14 and became a familiar sight in their back row, wearing the No. 13 shirt. He was said throughout his playing career to be utterly fearless, which was entirely in keeping with a man who once landed a Sopwith Pup aircraft on the flight deck of HMS *Vindictive* in the space of 60 yards, the only pilot known to have done so.

As a player, Wakefield quickly established a reputation as a dribbler of the ball and a hard scrummager, but he was also a fine handler and distributor. He was of rangy build, which ideally suited him as a forward, but he was still fast enough to play on the wing, a position he often occupied if a player was injured.

They like to tell the story at Sedbergh of Wakefield, clad
in three or four sweaters, running over the fells in weather
so fearsomely cold that the hair on his legs became encrusted
with icicles. They believed then that those experiences
helped to mould, discipline and strengthen a fine character
without any loss of enterprise or individualism.

Wakefield captained every team he ever played for. This
represented a fair spread, because his teams included
Sedbergh, Harlequins, Leicester, Pembroke College, Cambridge, Cambridge University, the Royal Air Force,
England, the Barbarians and Middlesex.

In January 1920, then aged 21, Wakefield broke into the
England side for the first time and was one of eleven new
caps to play against Wales at Swansea, the Welsh winning
19–5. By the time Wakefield played his final game, against
France in Paris in 1927, he had achieved more than enough
to become a legend in English rugby. His 31 appearances
stood as a record for 42 years until the total was overtaken
by Budge Rogers, the Bedford back-row forward. In every
position in the England team, with the exception of full back
and scrum-half, Wakefield's tally has since been equalled or
beaten; but his caps were all won during a period when
international rugby was a fairly limited activity with nothing
like the opportunities which exist today.

The Grand Slam in the international championship means
beating all other four competing countries, and Wakefield
played in three different years of triumph, 1921, 1923 and
1924. He was appointed captain for the first time in 1924 and
led the side in 13 matches, a figure which was equalled by
Nim Hall from 1949–53, Eric Evans from 1956–8, Dickie
Jeeps from 1960–2, and John Pullin from 1972–5, before
Bill Beaumont, with 21 matches as captain from 1978–82,
eclipsed them all.

Wakefield's family motto – "Be Just and Fear Not" –
would aptly have described his time with England. His first
two Grand Slam seasons were under the captaincy of fly-half
W. J. A. Davies and included the game at Twickenham in

1923 when Wakefield kicked off against Wales into a strong wind. "In case I mis-kicked I had Leo Price on my left," Wakefield wrote later. "I did mis-kick slightly and Price, following up, caught the ball, took a drop at goal, but the ball blew back again. Price caught it once more and scored under the posts. No Welshman had touched the ball and I was running alongside him shouting "'Pass, pass, pass'." England won 7–3.

Wakefield played through a wonderfully emotive period of English rugby. Twickenham had been opened in 1910 and, by the time Wakefield came into the England team, he was to play with some of the great forwards of the twenties, including Tommy Voyce of Gloucester, Arthur Blakiston, Geoff Conway – also renowned as a dribbler – and Ronald Cove-Smith, as well as Davies and Cecil "K" Kershaw, at half back, and the wing C. N. "Kid" Lowe whose 25 matches were consecutive and spanned the First World War. The King was a regular visitor to Twickenham, which now bulged with capacity attendances, and even after Wakefield had departed from the side the decade was to produce one more Grand Slam, in 1928.

Cove-Smith was in command for this campaign – four years earlier he had captained the British Lions in South Africa, a tour in which Wakefield did not take part – but from 1932 the Grand Slam was no longer an option after matches were halted against France because of allegations of professionalism. France returned to the championship in 1947 and, almost ten months after England had beaten them 6–3 at Twickenham, the name of Eric Evans of Sale appeared in the England side for the first time.

Evans played at prop against Australia, who won 11–0. Evans had to wait two more years before he was chosen again, this time as hooker, in a side which lost to Wales 5–11; he was promptly dropped for a second time. At last, in 1951, Evans began the long-term incumbency which was to lead to England's first post-War Grand Slam, in 1957.

Four years earlier England had taken the championship

outright for the first time since 1937 but this success was not backed up, and when Evans was given the leadership in 1956 there were ten new caps for him to introduce to the rigours of international football. The following year, when the Slam was won, there was just one.

By the time he began his 13–match run as captain, Evans was almost 35 years old. As a boy at Audeshaw Grammar School, he had been frustrated in his ambition to play soccer for Manchester United. He had been a useful soccer player at the Manchester Road council school and turned out for Droylsdon Boys as a right wing. "It broke my heart when I went to the grammar school because I had to play rugby there," he recalled. "I cried like a big soft kid to my father because I was a dyed-in-the-wool soccer player. But it was the best thing I ever did."

Evans played for Old Aldwinians before joining Sale in 1945 and staying with them until he retired in 1962. Like Wavell Wakefield, Evans captained all the sides he played for and was such an experienced player by the time he led England that he had few qualms.

It has to be remembered that in those days the captain ran the entire England performance. He organized the pre-match practice and virtually everything else until the team broke up after a cocktail party on the morning after the match.

Evans sent a personal letter to each player when he was appointed captain. He told them it was the most wonderful thing in the world to represent one's country and urged them all to train harder than ever before.

Curiously his fame in rugby allowed him to build a link with Manchester United. He began to train with the club as often as he could and developed a keen admiration for the way they worked. For three, perhaps four years, Evans ran with the footballers and just hoped that the players in the England team would know what he meant when he said: "You can only run as fast as the people who are with you."

In 1958 Manchester United were flying home from a European Cup match when their aircraft crashed on take-off at

21

Munich airport. Evans knew everyone in their squad and was numbed by the deaths and injury to players who had shared their professionalism with him, an amateur. He went to all the funerals and read lessons at some of them.

Evans was more anxious than he cared to admit when he was made captain. Even though he had been through it all before as a player, traces of doubt had crossed his mind about whether his players would be as committed as the Irish or the Welsh of the day.

Indeed, his first match as captain ended in defeat by 3–8 to Wales at Twickenham. Evans reminded his players at half-time that if they wanted to go to Dublin for the next match they had better dig in and win. It made no difference. England won two matches in 1956 but Evans knew that his pack, which included Ron Jacobs, John Currie, David Marques, Peter Robbins, Alan Ashcroft and Reg Higgins, would be just that shade wiser in 1957.

It was Evans's father, Walter, a property owner, who had been responsible for the attitude Evans had in rugby. "Whenever I was dropped my father told me to go to bed early, train more, and if I was playing as well as my rivals I would go in because I would be fitter. My father used to watch me everywhere but usually he would walk away at the end and never gave me praise. 'Just get stuck in,' he'd say."

During the training sessions Evans asked his players to make sure they reacted to situations quickly. An emotional man, he was not afraid to cry like a baby when the mood took him; but he and his men created a belief that they could not be beaten over the short but demanding haul of the championship.

Evans knew he could count on his forwards. "There were no big heads in the backs and they all knew their jobs. Dickie Jeeps was a cocky scrum-half but I wanted a straight feed from him and I wanted it timed right and he did that perfectly. Ricky Bartlett was an under-rated fly-half and all the other backs could play with him. We had Peter Jackson on the wing and I still believe now he never knew how good

22

he was. They did as I asked. I weighed only 12st. at the time but they listened to me. I suppose I had a bit of experience and personality and that counted for a lot."

The first match of the 1957 campaign was at Cardiff. It was settled by a single penalty from Fenwick Allison, the England full back, after half an hour and England managed to preserve that narrow lead for the rest of the game.

Next Evans took his men to Dublin and the character he knew existed within the team came to the fore when Peter Thompson, the Headingly wing, broke a rib after 23 minutes. That meant detaching Ashcroft from the pack and England's seven forwards clinging on. Jackson scored the only try, running back a missed touch kick by Ireland, and Bob Challis kicked a penalty.

Jackson scored two tries in the game against France at Twickenham, the first by twisting and turning through the defence, and the second through open space. To settle the game 9–5 Evans scored a try early in the second half and that touch-down in the south-west corner put England within one victory of the Grand Slam.

The last match, against Scotland, proved to be the easiest. The Queen and Prince Philip were among the crowd which saw England through by 16–3 and they watched as Evans was shouldered off at the end and on to a celebration dinner of Scotch broth, turbot, spring chicken and glazed pears. Only 17 players had appeared for England in the championship and the following morning they went to a cocktail party in Kensington little realizing that what they had done would not happen again to England for 23 years. The unfulfilled times were about to return.

CHAPTER 5

Eric Evans played on for another season, making his 30th and final appearance in March 1958, against Scotland. England retained the championship, but drawn matches with Wales and Scotland prevented an early repeat of the Grand Slam.

Wales were their first opponents and put in a rampaging forward performance at Twickenham under the leadership of Clem Thomas to remind the champions that they were in for a difficult season. Wales scored first with a penalty from Terry Davies, but England hit back in the second half with a try by Peter Thompson.

Evans was 37 on the day England played Australia. As England had not beaten one of the Southern Hemisphere countries since the War, there was considerable pressure on them to perform this time. Equally the Australians, who had already lost to Wales and Ireland, were in no mood to concede the match. A bitter contest resulted.

Fierce tackling cost England heavily. Phil Horrocks-Taylor, the fly-half, departed after 25 minutes with a leg injury. Jeff Butterfield, who moved from centre to fly-half, was affected by heavy tackling on three occasions and the bravery of England's new full-back, Jim Hetherington, a Cambridge blue, was unquestioned. No full-back relished a physical challenge more than Hetherington but he played much of this game concussed and at the finish had to be helped from the pitch.

England eventually won 9–6 after the Australians had twice been in front. Evans kept reminding his team of their qualities and their need to concentrate even more now that they were reduced to 14 players. The crowd, which resented Australia's physical approach, added greatly to England's cause.

Ironically it was the injury time which Australia inflicted on the game that produced the try which settled it in England's favour. Jackson was given the ball 25 yards out and in that short space was able to use most of his deceptive skills to score with a classic finishing dive.

Hetherington, now groggy, missed the conversion attempt, but nothing was going to change the state of play and the match went to its finish with Twickenham roaring England home. Evans and his men were left in a confident mood, but they had to play Ireland seven days later without Jackson, who was injured. This let into the team a phenomenally strong sprinter, John Young of Oxford University, for his first cap.

Ireland brought experience with them by the truckload. Under Noel Henderson's captaincy they had an impressive back division which included Jackie Kyle playing his 45th match at fly-half and a pack which contained men who would become hard-core British Lions – Ronnie Dawson, who was to lead the Lions to New Zealand in 1959, Gordon Wood, Bill Mulcahy and Noel Murphy.

In the heavy going there was not much open play and England won 6–0 on the strength of a penalty by Hetherington and a try by Ashcroft. This was a disappointing performance for England but they expressed themselves much more clearly in the game which followed against France, winning 14–0 in Paris, and scoring three tries, two by Thompson and another by Jackson, who covered two-thirds of the pitch to score.

So Evans prepared for his final match. With him in the side which played Scotland were eleven of the team which had clinched the Grand Slam the previous year and they looked strong enough to beat the Scots. However, many England teams have gone to Edinburgh with the label of favourites only to come unstuck, and this one suffered as well. Scotland, playing above their known form, shared the match 3–3.

In 1959 the captaincy switched to Butterfield, at centre. England did not score a try in four matches and scored only nine points in three games, almost unthinkable these days. It was a rapid testimony that all the authority generated in the 1957 Grand Slam had begun to evaporate.

Evans moved on to become an England selector, a job he liked far less than playing. Butterfield joined him on the selection panel a few years later and they were both selectors when England staged their first squad training session in December 1966.

Evans had been advocating this type of preparation for some time. In January 1966 he wrote: "I believe that a game is won months before it is played by getting oneself mentally attuned to the feeling that you are going to win and that you are never going to allow any Englishman to be messed about by anybody. This is the first thing we have to get right. How we do this I think is difficult but I'm prepared to admit that the good-looking fellow with lots of technical ability is not going to be good enough, particularly as a forward, to stand up to the Welsh miner who has got the heart and the mental drive to supersede his local form."

England's low scoring in 1959 still left them in joint second place in the championship, but in terms of winning places on the Lions tour to Australia and New Zealand that summer England did less well. Five players were chosen in the backs – Jackson, Butterfield, Jeeps, Young and Bev Risman, a fly-half – and just two forwards, Marques and Ashcroft.

It was a Lions tour to cherish, as well. The team won two Tests in Australia and only lost the first against New Zealand by 17–18 despite having scored four tries. But Don Clarke, a 16st. full-back, kicked six penalties for New Zealand to win the match at Dunedin.

The fifties had been a decade of no great change in the established order of rugby; but the sixties were to alter all that.

CHAPTER 6

For their first match in 1960, against Wales at Twickenham, England chose a full-back from the club in Northumberland, Percy Park, named Don Rutherford. He was working as an auctioneer's clerk, his first job after leaving school, and quickly graduated to auctioneer, selling fish at the market at North Shields.

By the end of the decade the same Don Rutherford was appointed technical administrator of the Rugby Football Union and he was to remain in this role for 20 years before being retitled technical director. Rutherford was not only the longest-serving employee of the Rugby Football Union in modern times, he was also the most influential in the playing aspects of the game. In effect he was chief coach, but legislation prevented him as a paid official from actually running the England team as such.

None of this would have been particularly obvious to Rutherford when he was ushered into international rugby as one of seven new caps. Three of the other newcomers, Mike Weston, at centre, and two forwards, Stan Hodgson and Derek Morgan, were also from the North-East. Rutherford remembers feeling grateful that they were there.

In the end, on that January afternoon, Twickenham throbbed at the exploits of only one of the new men – Richard Sharp, a fair-haired, leggy Cornishman who had come in at fly-half at the last moment for Bev Risman. Wales had brought a considerable team, including seven of the 1959 British Lions, but were utterly confounded by the pace and deceptive running of Sharp. Dickie Jeeps, England's new captain, decided that Sharp was so confident that he would give him the ball as often as possible.

Inspired by their new fly-half, England led 14–0 at half-time with Jim Roberts, a wing who had his hair swept back as if permanently on the attack, scoring two tries. One followed a break by Sharp from half-way, the other came after clever play by Weston. Rutherford had begun the scoring with a penalty – but in the adulation over Sharp's debut merited little other comment.

The England team remained unchanged throughout the championship – the only time that had happened – but they had a much harder test in their next match, against Ireland, when they trailed 0–5 in the early stages. Sharp, well shackled, dropped a goal and England went on to win the match with a try from David Marques, the only one he scored for England in 23 appearances.

Next England drew 3–3 with France in Paris and again Sharp made his mark, laying on the only try by Weston. Rutherford's conversion attempt, which he regarded as a sitter, hit the post and cost England victory. Prior to that, Michel Vannier had missed a few kicks for France and Rutherford has since been unfairly blamed for causing England to miss out on a Grand Slam. England staged a three-try finale to the championship by beating Scotland 21–12 at Murrayfield, so winning the Triple Crown for the first time since 1957.

Before the 1961 championship began, England played South Africa at Twickenham. In those days the game was structured so as to emphasize strength and size to the detriment of mobility, and South Africa more than lived up to the demand to produce a huge pack. Led by the Transvaal lock Avril Malan and containing other formidably large forwards in the tight five such as Fanie Kuhn, Piet du Toit and the immense Johan Claassen, these Springboks were quite prepared to grind out victories and take as few chances as possible.

This was exactly how they played England, and their force told in the end. They won by 5–0. The only score involved a drive by one of the most expansive of the Springboks, their No. 8, Doug Hopwood, and England had no chances at all. This match also marked the end of the record-breaking second-row partnership for England of David Marques and John Currie. For the following game, against Wales, Currie was forced to withdraw because of illness and Marques was dropped after one more match. They had played 22 consecutive matches together, an endurance test of both fitness and ability.

The 1961 championship provided a classic case of England dithering over who was their best fly-half. They had the choice between Sharp, with his flamboyance and elegant play, or Risman, a shorter, more compact player but equally effective at making breaks. They began with Risman, then moved him to centre with Sharp at fly-half. That lasted for two matches until Risman saved England any further argument by turning professional with Leigh in the Rugby League.

In 1962 there was not only a championship to play for but places on the Lions tour to South Africa that summer. England had two drawn games, against Wales and Scotland, but beat Ireland 16–0 with Sharp having an outstanding match, scoring one try and making another. However, in Paris Michel Crauste scored a hat trick of tries for France, a post-War record, and England did not respond.

Jeeps was definitely in the frame to captain the Lions but England's record in 1962 did not help him. Instead the Lions turned to the Scottish wing, Arthur Smith, who had led his side to within one victory of the Triple Crown, the frustration being the 3–3 draw with England at Murrayfield.

Smith and his Lions played 24 matches in South Africa, but after drawing the first Test 3–3 were beaten in the next three Tests. Jeeps, on his third Lions tour, played in all four Tests and retired with a record at that time of 13 Test appearances. He was to go on to become a selector, president of the Rugby Football Union and chairman of the Sports Council.

Sharp and the Scot, Gordon Waddell, were the fly-half choices for the Lions. In the seventh game, against Northern Transvaal at Pretoria, Sharp was put off the pitch after only five minutes by a late tackle by Mannie Roux. Sharp's cheekbone was fractured and he remained in hospital until after the second Test.

As Hodgson, the England hooker, had broken his leg in the first match of the tour, two of the ten England players who represented the Lions suffered badly. Sharp recovered in time to be in contention for the third and fourth Tests and won the place over Waddell. It was to be Sharp's only Lions tour.

It was also the last Lions tour to travel without an official coach; already there were moves for and resistance against the introduction of coaching to British and Irish rugby and there were important steps in that direction in 1964. Before that came a match which was to prove a watershed in the long history of English rugby. The game was Wales v England, at Cardiff on 19 January 1963.

Sharp took over the England captaincy from Jeeps. The side which he took to Cardiff contained six new caps in the pack and a new scrum-half in Simon Clarke of Cambridge University. Jackson, who had been in the wilderness, was recalled to the wing at the age of 32.

Wales regarded the match as one they should have won. They had a thread of experience through the team and could vary things at half back through the kicking of Clive Rowlands, the scrum-half and captain, and David Watkins, the supremely gifted fly-half from Newport. Whatever the pre-match speculation everyone at the Arms Park that day remembers how cold it was and how hard was the pitch.

Roberts touched off the first score following a line-out. He

31

saw Weston in the middle of the pitch as he was about to throw in and accurately put the ball into Weston's hands. Weston, then Phillips, and finally Jackson worked the ball upfield and Phillips regained possession to score. In the second half Phillips was involved again when John Owen, one of the new forwards, scored England's second try and, with Sharp converting twice and dropping a goal, England won 13–6.

Nobody in the ground that day or the thousands more who watched the spectacle on television could have realized that a great dead hand was to descend over England following their performance. Nobody took much notice when England did not win again at Cardiff in the sixties but gradually the record became worse and worse. Through the seventies, at the height of the latest Welsh golden era, the gaps became embarrassingly wide. There was a draw in 1983, but the eighties passed without an England victory.

Of course the burden was on England to break the mould and the more they failed to do so the harder was the task for the players who succeeded them. It held back England's development, and they were capable, as a result, of losing to almost any Welsh side, and not only at Cardiff. England would deny that they froze mentally against Wales but there was plenty of evidence to suggest that they did, none more so than in the quarter-final of the 1987 World Cup in Brisbane.

Curiously, the matches became a burden for Wales as well. No Welsh player wanted to be part of the first Welsh side to lose to England at Cardiff since 1963, and the pressures on those players were felt just as keenly as they were in the English squad. Some bitter matches resulted, clear evidence that rugby football at this level cannot always keep itself in check when the build-up has been so intense.

Winning so regularly against England at Cardiff may also have spoiled Wales from advancing as much as they might have liked. Sometimes the England match seemed to be the only one which mattered, as though beating England was enough to paper over the cracks of an otherwise thin year.

32

Clive Rowlands and Roger Michaelson were the two Welsh players from the 1963 game who had good cause to hope that England might win one day. Rowlands was labelled as the last Welsh captain to lose to England at Cardiff and Michaelson, a No. 8 from Aberavon who is street-market fluent in both French and Spanish, won his only cap in the 1963 game.

Much later, after New Zealand had beaten Wales when he was managing the team in the first World Cup, Rowlands referred to the future by underlining that, if nothing else, Wales would want to go on beating England year by year. As Wales had finished in third place and England had long gone home to lick their wounds Rowlands could have been accused of lacking ambition; however it summed up a sad truth that the England match at Cardiff had become an obsession.

After the 1963 game, Wales went on to take the wooden spoon. England followed with a draw against Ireland, beat France 6–5 and in the last match against Scotland found themselves 0–8 behind.

Sharp and Jackson brought England back by setting up a move from which Nick Drake-Lee scored a try. Then Sharp, with a magnificent solo try after a run which confused at least three key Scottish defenders, levelled the scores and the conversion by John Willcox put England 10–8 ahead, a margin they sustained until the end.

England had won the title outright for the last time for 17 years on 16 March 1963. It was two weeks after that final game that Bill and Pam Carling were married at St Mary Abbotts Church in High Street Kensington, West London.

CHAPTER 7

It would be wrong to say that coaching did not arrive in English rugby, or anywhere else in British and Irish rugby, until the sixties. Players had always been involved in coaching their own teams since the game began and were doing so just as vigorously in the sixties. However, not until that decade did formal team coaches start to emerge.

The great English clubs, then as now, included Northampton, Coventry and Bristol, all of whom relied on the input from their large contingents of international players to produce high playing standards; but growing exposure to countries in the Southern Hemisphere showed the width of the gap between their standards and those in the home countries.

England decided to do something about it. During the 1963–4 season the Rugby Union set up a coaching committee. It was an opportune moment. England had won the championship but had been beaten twice by New Zealand and once by Australia on the first overseas tour that year. Early in 1964, as well, England were beaten 14–0 by New Zealand at Twickenham. By 1966 England had produced *A Guide for Coaches* which probably benefited many other countries as much as it did themselves.

In Wales, too, there was something of a rush to join the coaching revolution. This followed a match in Durban, in

May 1964, when Wales were beaten 24–3 by the Springboks who scored 21 points in the final quarter of the match. John Dawes, who was to go on to captain the 1971 British Lions in New Zealand, was in the Welsh team that day. Another player who watched from the stands was Ron Waldron, the Neath prop, who was to become team manager of Wales in 1990 after the side had suffered a new record 6–34 defeat against England at Twickenham.

Wales were horrified at the margin of defeat to South Africa and were determined to revamp their approach to the game. Three years later Ray Williams, a visionary coach who was responsible, among other things, for the creation of mini rugby for very young players, became coaching organizer to the Welsh Rugby Union.

Another Welshman, John Robins, was appointed coach to the 1966 British Lions for their tour to Australia and New Zealand. But Robins did not coach the squad or have the authority which a Lions coach would have today. Michael Campbell-Lamerton, an army officer and Scottish forward who was a surprise choice to lead that Lions tour, was determined to head the operation and it was not until the Lions went to South Africa in 1968, with Ronnie Dawson of Ireland as coach, that proper acknowledgement was given to the role.

Don Rutherford was one of the 1966 Lions. He wrote a report on what he observed on the tour and some of his opinions were contained in the ten pamphlets which formed *A Guide for Coaches*. Yet not until 1969, when Don White of Northampton was appointed, did England have a team coach.

England might have appeared to have had many problems in the sixties but the only record defeat they suffered in the decade was against Wales: 21–34 at Cardiff in 1967, when the outcome was greatly influenced by the 18-year-old schoolboy from Newport, Keith Jarrett. In his first match, at full back, Jarrett scored 19 points, beginning with a penalty after nine minutes which struck an upright and went over, and including

35

a try after he had gathered an English kick ahead and counter-attacked.

England had gone to Cardiff that day with the Triple Crown in their sights, knowing that the championship-winners would, depending on results, be drawn from England, Ireland or France. The French emerged as champions and England's next game was against New Zealand at Twickenham in November when Brian Lochore's team won 23–11 against an England side which relied heavily on players drawn from the Midlands.

This match with the All Blacks served as another reminder of what quality coaching could do for a side. Fred Allen was coach to the New Zealand squad and made the highest of demands on fitness, work rate, ball use, and support play. He had a marvellously equipped team to develop his ideals and, but for being prevented from travelling to Ireland because of an outbreak of foot and mouth disease, those All Blacks might have achieved a Grand Slam against the home countries. Lochore, modest and shrewd as a captain, was to have his day as a coach much later – in preparing New Zealand to win the inaugural World Cup in 1987.

The Lions did not win a Test match in 12 attempts against South Africa and New Zealand in the sixties, and when the side led by the Irish full back Tom Kiernan returned from South Africa in 1968 the tour manager, David Brooks, a London fruit importer, began to beat the drum around England for competition to become an organized part of English rugby. His pleas fell for the most part on deaf ears. It was a further four years before England introduced a Cup competition, another 19 before the clubs of England eventually formed themselves into nationwide leagues.

However, at international level England were stirring. For the first time players involved in England trials were asked to stay on and practice the following day. Dick Greenwood, who would emerge later as an England coach, during his brief period as captain persuaded the players to meet at their own expense for additional training.

Finally the Rugby Union decided that England should have a coach. Following the 1969 match in Cardiff, when Wales won 30–9 and Maurice Richards scored a record-equalling four tries, and after a season which saw the emergence of John Spencer and David Duckham as a potentially thrilling centre pairing, England set up a 30-strong squad four months ahead of the game with South Africa in December. And Don White was invited to become the coach.

That White was the first England coach was no surprise. He was then aged 43 and had long been regarded as one of the foremost thinkers on the game. He was born in the Northamptonshire village of Earls Barton, where he now heads the family footwear business, and has had a lifelong connection with the Northampton club.

White played in the England back row between 1947 and 1952, winning 14 caps, and remained in club rugby until 1961. He was fortunate enough to play in some creative teams but would be the first to admit that he owed much of his thinking to an Australian obstetrician, Gordon Sturtridge, who was connected with Northampton for almost 30 years.

The side which eventually took the field against South Africa on 20 December 1969 contained five players who were either past or future England captains. In the second row was Mike Davis who would move on to become England's Grand Slam coach in 1980.

White could see that he had plenty of experience around him, which was just as well because he chose five new caps for the game, including the half-backs, Roger Shackleton and Nigel Starmer-Smith. Playing against South Africa, even though the match was at Twickenham, was a daunting start for any England player.

This was no straightforward tour by the Springboks. They arrived for their tour of Britain and Ireland full of promise and unsuspecting of the difficulties which lay ahead. For this was the first South African tour to feel the considerable weight of anti-apartheid protest. Somehow the Springboks played through it, but they have not been invited back. History was also made on that tour: England beat South Africa for the first time.

CHAPTER 8

The South African tour stretched from October 1969 into February 1970, and if protesters were not properly geared up when Dawie de Villiers, the captain, arrived with his players they were very soon afterwards. It was a unique tour with anti-apartheid demonstrators present at many of the 25 matches, some of which were disrupted by pitch invasions. The game at Bristol against Western Counties was held up for a while after an intruder threw tin tacks on to the pitch.

Rugby officials in England, Ireland, Scotland and Wales were determined that the tour should go ahead as planned, and mostly it did. The opening match was due to be at the University ground in Oxford but the police felt that they could not guarantee smooth progress and a last-minute change of venue took the game to Twickenham.

The Rugby Union allowed spectators to use only one of the four sides of the ground and the match was played to a cacophony of whistles from the demonstrators and with a police presence numbering more than four hundred. Many of the other matches were played to a similar background, except that this one brought a defeat for the Springboks, Oxford, led by the New Zealand scrum-half Chris Laidlaw, beating them 6–3.

At the sharp end of the demonstrators in England was an organization known as the "Stop the Seventy Tour" whose aim was to force cancellation of the 1970 South African cricket tour. It was obvious to anyone who saw the disruption at rugby matches that cricket would be impossible under similar conditions. The rugby tour was played out to the end – with one substitute fixture for the one originally planned against Ulster in Belfast – but the cricket tour did not take place. No South African national side, at any sport, has come to Britain since.

In terms of results the tour was a disaster for the South Africans. They were beaten by both Scotland and England and drew with Ireland and Wales, but it was a tribute to the character of the Springboks that they stuck to it and even finished with a triumphant 21–12 win over the Barbarians at Twickenham on 31 January 1970, the last time the famed green shirt was seen in Britain.

Eight English teams played the South Africans. The national side were the only winners but there were close results almost everywhere, including a 3–3 draw with Western Counties. Some of the English opposition included unheralded players such as Tony Neary, a flanker in the North West Counties side, and Roger Uttley, a lock in the North East Counties team.

Don White had been appointed England coach at the suggestion of Albert Agar, a banker who was then chairman of the selectors. The invitation appealed to White and he instituted Sunday training sessions at a variety of grounds. He assumed that the players would take care of their own fitness routines because he wanted to concentrate entirely on teamwork.

"We worked hard in those sessions, getting our scrum right, working on rucks and mauls, and getting the backs functioning," White says. "Roger Shackleton was going to be our fly-half and I remember telling him that I wouldn't say when he should kick, that was his judgement, but not to overkick because we needed a balanced game. I tried to ensure that we had tacklers in the backs and eight forwards who were able to live with the Springboks. I had played against South Africa in 1951–2 and again in 1960 so the selection philosophy from those days was in my mind.

"I knew that the demonstrations against them would not be helping them but that was their problem. You cannot fight other people's battles. I have always believed in playing football and felt that you cannot play against the best unless you play balanced rugby. If you don't give the backs the ball, how crazy can it be? The backs will never have confidence to do things under pressure unless they have the ball."

White and the selectors chose the team to face South Africa and the five new caps already knew that they would be playing with a new captain, Bob Hiller, a full back from Harlequins who had played on the wing for London against the Springboks earlier in the tour. Hiller was a fabulous goal kicker, one of the last great toe-end kickers, and in all led England in seven matches. Yet only twice did he finish in a winning side.

England went two scores down, 0–8, in the first half, but the new half backs, Starmer-Smith and Shackleton, broke out to the Springbok line and as the forwards came up in support Peter Larter, a giant lock forward, scored in the corner.

This try was perfectly timed to lift England's effort, and Hiller emphasized the potential prize when he spoke to his forwards at half time. All the players, and then the crowd, captured the mood. Midway through the second half Hiller cut the South African lead to two points with a penalty and England finally took the lead for the first time ten minutes from time with a controversial score. The ball came out on the South African side of a maul, on their own line, and the contest to touch down first lay between Pullin, the England hooker, and de Villiers. Pullin thought de Villiers took his eye off the ball to check where his fly-half was. Pullin dived and was awarded the try, the only one he scored for England in 42 matches – and what a precious score it was. Hiller converted but was to miss the closing moments of his historic leadership because of a hip injury. Even so, the deed had been done – 11–8 to England.

The South Africans had lost the first two Tests of the tour and British supporters were optimistic that maybe Wales and Ireland could add to their miseries. For a while there was even a suggestion that the Springboks would return early because of an incident which preceded the England game when a demonstrator entered a coach carrying reserves and supporters and chained himself to the steering wheel. The Springbok manager, Corrie Bornman, complained about this at the England match dinner and said the next day that the future of the tour depended on them being assured by the authorities that they were not in danger of injury or death. That assurance was given, and the tour rolled on.

For White, the England coaching show was now firmly on the road but after the same side which had beaten South Africa also defeated Ireland, inexplicably the regular training sessions were ended.

When Wales came to Twickenham, White reasoned that Gareth Edwards, the Welsh captain and scrum-half, would be the player to check and the more Edwards was stopped the more he would want to prove England wrong. White felt that if Edwards could be upset or closed down, then the supply of the ball to the great creator in the Welsh team, Barry John at fly-half, would be reduced. Sure enough, Edwards was bottled up by the England plan; but he was injured early, Wales brought on Chico Hopkins at scrum-half who presented an entirely different obstacle, and Wales won. Defeat to Scotland meant that England finished the season by dropping Hiller as captain and full back in one of six changes for the visit to France, who gleefully took on an inexperienced side to win by 35–12 and make everyone wonder whether coaching was a worthwhile exercise or not.

In 1971, England's centenary year, the championship began with yet another defeat at Cardiff. Hiller was recalled to score all the points in a win over Ireland and a draw with France, but then Scotland won at Twickenham for the first

42

time since the War and won again seven days later in the special centenary match at Murrayfield.

White stood down after two seasons. He had been the first coach and England have maintained the post ever since; but not all the best and most successful club coaches have been in demand for the national job – Jack Rowell of Bath, Chalky White of Leicester and Alan Davies of Nottingham being just three examples.

In 1983 Don White joined the Rugby Football Union committee as the representative for East Midlands. He now believes it is unhealthy for coaches to have too much power, particularly as the game heads towards professional coaching.

"The situation will be that they will be driving amateurs to keep them in a professional job. If the game proceeds as it is there will be another split off [as there was when the Rugby League was formed] and there will be professional Rugby Union and amateur Rugby Union administered by different people. I don't believe either that you can play Rugby Union professionally to our current laws. The game will have to evolve as Rugby League has evolved to stop the ball after tackles to cut out the danger. I don't think we can allow the game to go professional at the top and keep the same laws.

"When money is involved people become even more ruthless. I joined the Rugby Football Union hoping to stem what I could see as a rush into professionalism, because I thought it would spoil the game. I did hope that I could keep the game a players' game for enjoyment and not one that would be stress from one week to the next. Now we don't play for enjoyment, we play to win. It's probably gone too far to draw the line where I hoped to draw the line, and I believe there will be a split.

"Nothing changes about playing the game, about putting pressure on good players opposite you. That's the captain's job to do that, to try out where pressure succeeds and to keep pressurizing.

"When England play well I love it. At their best they are

an absolute joy to watch. They fall down when they can't change their ideas when something isn't working."

White handed over the England coaching job to John Elders, a schoolmaster from Northumberland. Elders had a miserable start. The 1972 championship in which England used two captains, Bob Hiller and Peter Dixon, and did not play the same team twice in the four matches, ended with four defeats, the first time that had happened.

There was an air of despair after the fourth defeat, at Murrayfield, which has rarely been equalled in the long history of English rugby. It was during or just after that weekend that an approach was made to John Pullin to ask him to captain the side.

CHAPTER 9

John Vivian Pullin has not strayed far from his birthplace in Aust, almost on the eastern shore of the Severn Estuary. Once the main road outside his house carried the traffic to the Aust-to-Beachley ferry service but now the Severn Bridge does that task and Pullin, who farms sheep and dairy cattle, has relative peace.

Yet it was from this secluded base in the West Country that Pullin stepped forward to play international rugby from 1966–76. He played for England in 42 Test matches at hooker – a record. Thirty-six of those caps were in succession, which is also a record, and he had 13 matches as captain. All of this followed a disastrous start for Pullin when he was dropped after his debut against Wales in 1966 and not selected again for two years.

None of this mattered a great deal to the young Pullin when he set off for Thornbury Grammar School having passed his eleven plus examination. It was that school which introduced him to rugby. He began as a hooker and never played in any other position.

The first selectors to take notice of him were the men who chose the Bristol Public and Grammar Schools team. After school, Pullin went on to the Bristol Saracens club, beginning in the fourth team, and had his chance eventually in the first team when the regular choice was injured.

Next came an invitation to play for Bristol, and although Pullin knew that the club hooker was John Thorne, also an England player, he had no hesitation in moving on. Thorne too was injured and Bristol put the young Pullin into the club front row. His first match was against Newport, whose hooker was Bryn Meredith. Bristol told Pullin that Meredith was a Lion but the term meant nothing to him. Pullin won a strike against the head for John Blake to drop a goal and win the game, and it was then that someone explained that Meredith was part of the famed 1955 British Lions front row in South Africa.

Pullin's next club match was against Cardiff, who had an international hooker in Billy Thomas. Then came Swansea, who also had an international hooker in Norman Gale. He learned fast.

In this initial burst of activity for Bristol, Pullin played 14 games in a row and had begun to fancy his chances. The 15th game was at Northampton and brought Pullin into conflict with Andy Johnson who had already played for England Schools and had a growing reputation. Pullin soon discovered why, as Johnson relieved him of 14 Bristol put-ins. Pullin was dropped, but recovered. To his amazement Johnson was never capped at senior level. "I always had the greatest respect for him," Pullin says now. "Andy Johnson was the best – streets ahead of anyone else. He was a very clever and fast hooker."

Pullin went on, winning his first cap after playing three trials in the junior side, and surviving being dropped after his opening game which was against Wales and Norman Gale. In England's next nine matches there were two wins only. The defeats included those against Australia and New Zealand in 1967. The All Blacks scored 18 points before half time.

When England started their 1968 season Pullin was among the men charged with correcting things. Two draws and a win helped, and Pullin was selected for that year's Lions tour to South Africa, along with seven other English players.

Pullin's rival for the Test place in South Africa was Jeff Young of Wales. There was never much doubt, though, that Pullin would be first choice, and despite the fact that injury had ruled him out for the first Test he played the other three.

At some stage of the second Test Pullin wondered why he had gone to South Africa at all. He had never experienced opposing forward pressure such as the Springboks mounted that day. "You found yourself wondering if your arm might break and you could go off," he says. "They were so strong they just put you where they wanted and you couldn't move your feet. I learned more in South Africa in 1968 than anywhere else."

The Lions drew that Test in Port Elizabeth, but were beaten in the other three. England's Lions came home and had poor reward from their own selectors – Hiller, Pullin and Larter were the only Lions to start the championship with England the following year.

Pullin played on and on for England, under different captains and with varying results, and in 1971 was chosen for the Lions for a second time, for the visit to New Zealand. Peter Dixon, a back-row forward, was the only other England forward to be an initial choice for the tour while England provided three backs – Hiller, David Duckham and John Spencer.

The Lions tour was headed by a Welsh captain in John Dawes and a Welsh coach in Carwyn James. It might have been a small English contingent but Pullin played all four Tests in New Zealand, Dixon three and Duckham three, while Hiller kept kicking goals in every team he played for.

The Lions won the first and third Tests, lost the second and drew the last. This was a time when global communications were not as sophisticated as they are today but the message came thundering home from New Zealand week by week that the 1971 Lions were special.

They had J.P.R. Williams and Gerald Davies and Duckham and Dawes and Mike Gibson in the backs, with Barry John and Gareth Edwards at half back, and they had

47

steel and experience all the way through the forwards in the shape of men like Willie John McBride, Mervyn Davies, Pullin and John Taylor as well as a couple of emerging props in Sean Lynch and Ian "Mighty Mouse" McLauchlan. These six forwards played in all four Tests.

By producing a series victory in New Zealand, the 1971 Lions made history ... and made it all the harder for their successors. There have been two tours since, in 1977 and 1983, but it was the 1971 men who captured the imagination and came home to unprecedented scenes of welcome.

When the players resumed with their own countries, it was England who stumbled alarmingly with those unprecedented four defeats in the championship. In came Pullin as captain and his first mission was to lead England on their first tour of South Africa. Pullin had no worries about the task, because he remembered what he had learned in South Africa in 1968 and what it was like to beat the Springboks at Twickenham in 1969. His experiences in New Zealand had taught him a lot more about the attitude of the Southern Hemisphere player and he was ready to pass on his knowledge.

England were the last of the home countries to visit South Africa. The Springboks had beaten Ireland, Scotland and Wales in the sixties with something to spare, had won two Test series against the Lions and seen off France and New Zealand as well. Pullin was still not worried.

Alec Lewis, whose service to rugby is so tireless that he can now be found cheerfully helping supporters into the car park at the Bath club, was the manager for the tour and believed his players could win all seven matches which faced them. So did John Elders, the coach. They were not far wrong – one game was drawn.

Pullin's experience as captain was extremely limited. He remembered captaining a second team at school – and also remembered that privilege being removed because he had been caught smoking. But the man the players called "Piggy" quickly won their interest and loyalty.

The only Test of the tour was to be played at the Ellis

48

Park stadium in Johannesburg, which is almost 6,000 feet above sea level. Victories over Natal and Western Province convinced Pullin and his men that they were on the right lines and they headed into the Test with four new caps. One was Sam Doble, the Moseley full back. Doble could kick the ball a long way but in the rarefied atmosphere of Johannesburg it seemed to travel for ever.

Pullin was propped by "Stack" Stevens, the Cornishman who had been a replacement on the 1971 Lions tour, and by Mike Burton. Pullin wanted Burton at tight head because the Gloucester man was such a good scrummager – and England needed to scrummage the Springboks.

Pullin was also pleased to have the long-serving Larter and the rising Chris Ralston at lock, together with Tony Neary and John Watkins on the flanks, both certain tacklers, and the unpredictable Andy Ripley and his astonishing pace at No. 8.

Pullin and his tight-five forwards did everything which was needed and the pace of the England pack to the loose ball was a significant factor. Jan Webster, the Moseley scrum half, was outstanding in only his third game for England and made the one try of the Test. He re-won his own kick ahead and put through the Bristol wing, Alan Morley, for a try. Doble converted and kicked four penalties and a massive crowd of more than 77,000 took a long time to realize that they had just witnessed history being made.

England flew home in high spirits. Nobody had given them much of a chance but they had won and they had laid the foundations for a promising future. Little did they realize what 1973 had in store for them.

CHAPTER 10

The plan was for England to play New Zealand once in 1973, at Twickenham. It was the 20th match of the All Blacks tour that winter and by that time Ian Kirkpatrick's New Zealanders had beaten Wales 19–16 and Scotland 14–9.

The New Zealanders had also lost three matches. In the highly emotional setting of Stradey Park they fell to Delme Thomas and his Llanelli team 3–9 in a game which ensured that every pub in the town, and a good many elsewhere, would be drunk dry.

From an English viewpoint the first key date of the tour was at Workington where North West Counties, led by Fran Cotton at prop, beat the tourists 16–14. This was a mammoth achievement because, apart from one loss to England, in 1936, the All Blacks had strode the country unbeaten for more than 60 years.

The success of the Lancashire side and their coach, John Burgess, was interwoven into the North West effort and reflected lengthy planning – the team first assembled in August for a match in November – and perfect execution. The North West won in the final minutes after being 12–14 behind, and suddenly a whole new group of players had a different understanding about the All Blacks.

One more English side was to experience the same feeling, Midland Counties West defeating the All Blacks 16–8 at

Moseley. But it is important to explain what happened in the four days before this game.

The previous Saturday, New Zealand had beaten Wales at Cardiff. At some stage during the Saturday night Keith Murdoch, the moustachioed All Blacks prop from Otago, had been involved in an altercation with a security guard in a hotel. The affair was debated by the All Blacks management over the weekend and on the Monday they decided that Murdoch should be dismissed from the tour. He came to London by train from Birmingham and the last that most people saw of Murdoch was at Euston station where he walked silently down the platform, his blazer stripped of its All Blacks silver fern badge, *en route* to a back room in a travel agent's office and ultimately a night flight from Heathrow.

Some of the All Blacks thought that Murdoch should not have been punished in this way. There was much bitterness in the party against the management and against British officials who were perceived to have been involved in the decision to send Murdoch home. The New Zealanders were off balance when they ran out at Moseley, and suffered for it. But by the time the All Blacks came to Twickenham they had won seven matches in a row and the rhythm and discipline were back in their play. Pullin had ten of the players who had won in South Africa in his side, but Cotton was a last-minute absentee and so was Alan Old, the fly-half.

New Zealand, playing to a predetermined plan involving their pack and scrum-half Sid Going, had two scores on the board in the first eight minutes, and when England missed four penalty attempts their chances began to fade. New Zealand won 9–0.

Pullin and another of his England team, David Duckham, were to have another chance at the All Blacks in the tour finale at Cardiff when the Barbarians chose a particularly skilled and experienced side, many of whom had been Lions in New Zealand in 1971. It was billed as the revenge match for British and Irish rugby and in many ways it was, because

51

the All Blacks had been deprived of a Grand Slam only by a surprise 10–10 draw with Ireland.

The Barbarians called in the Lions coach, Carwyn James, to help prepare the side. John Dawes, the Lions captain, was given the leadership. Familiarity bred confidence, even though it was nearly two years since the players had been together. The Barbarians, through Gareth Edwards, scored one of their greatest tries (and certainly one of the most widely broadcast) to set them on their way and led, staggeringly, by 17–0 at half-time. The closing score was 17–11 which said much for the attitude of the New Zealanders and even more about the Barbarians in holding them out. Pullin could afford to smile to himself. He had done it again.

Now the 1973 championship beckoned. In 1972 the championship was not completed because both Scotland and then Wales decided not to travel to Dublin to play against Ireland because of the violence in Ulster and possible threats against them if they appeared at Lansdowne Road. Neutral venues were suggested and rejected. In 1972 Ireland played two games in the championship, both away, and won in Paris for the first time for 20 years and at Twickenham for only the third time since the War. It was not difficult to imagine how despondent the Irish felt about the unfulfilled matches.

England were due to play in Dublin on 10 February 1973, and the Rugby Football Union committee made it clear some time ahead that the fixture would be fulfilled. Pullin and Sandy Sanders, the chairman of selectors, had driven back together from the Welsh match at Cardiff in January and Pullin said firmly that he was not worried about going to Dublin and neither were his players. Pullin felt that the Rugby Union would take a team to Dublin, no matter how many dropped out, and he was determined to play. Only two of the likely England team were not available.

The players were told that they would be subjected to intense security from the start of their journey to its finish and the heavy police presence when they arrived in Dublin assured them of this. They stayed in the same hotel as the opposition and there was no doubt that there was more than the usual tension in the team as the match approached.

The return of international rugby to Dublin for the first time for two years was marked by a clever touch by the Irish Rugby Union. Either they sent England out on to the pitch a little earlier than planned or they delayed the arrival of the Irish team, but it meant that England were given a colossal welcome as they took the field. They had rarely been applauded like it, even at Twickenham, and it would be true to say that ever since England have felt more welcome in Dublin than any of the other grounds they visit regularly.

For anyone who played for England, and for those who watched, it was one of the most emotional of days. At the after-match dinner Pullin commented: "We may not be the best team in the world but at least we turn up." Ireland loved Pullin for that. Ireland also loved the game. They won it 18–9.

The 1973 championship ended with a five way split because for the first time each country won two home matches. England's win over France at Twickenham ended a sequence of seven defeats in a row in the championship, their worst ever. The only newcomer to the England pack that season was Roger Uttley, who began in Dublin, playing in the second row.

In the summer of 1973 England were due to tour Argentina for the first time, but there were threats from guerrilla groups against the players and the tour was cancelled. In its place the Rugby Union arranged a tour to Fiji, with one match against the national team in Suva, and to New Zealand, with one match against the All Blacks in Auckland preceded by three games against provincial opposition. Once more Pullin and the All Blacks were to test each other.

Fiji came first. England had stayed in training for the tour to Argentina and the change meant they were going to take on known opposition in unfamiliar places. By the time they landed at Nadi and took the short flight across to Suva they

53

had been travelling for more than 24 hours . . . and the first match was only four days away.

The players had insufficient time to recover from the flights and Fiji's ever-varying climate created further problems. But Pullin took the squad out to one of the little islands for a barbecue and reminded the players that although the setting might be unusual, this was where their rugby season was about to begin.

There was much confidence among England's runners because they had won the special Scottish centenary seven-a-side tournament at Murrayfield (beating Ireland in the final) and the belief was that good old-fashioned English discipline and tackling would tie the Fijians down and put them off their game.

An international match in Suva is something of an experience and an international match against England was even more special, but only a late try by Peter Squires, the Yorkshire wing, gave England victory by 13–12. No caps were awarded, which was a little tough on Peter Hendy, a farmer from the Lizard and a flanker from the St Ives club in Cornwall, who was the only uncapped player in the side.

England had little time to celebrate. The post-match activities included a visit to a club called "Man Friday's', and a variety of Fijian cocktails were tried during the night. Nevertheless there was a dawn start the next day for the final leg of the journey to New Zealand and a town called New Plymouth.

Pullin's team immediately found themselves up against good opposition who could draw crowds. They also found the rain and mud at New Plymouth more than a little exacting and, before a crowd of 17,000, lost to Taranaki 3–6.

Pullin stood down for the third game of the tour against Wellington, giving his place at hooker to his Bristol understudy John White. England once again disappointed, to lose 16–25. Three days later, against Canterbury at Christchurch, England scored three tries to lead one of New Zealand's top provinces, but they lost 12–19 and, with a week to go before they played the All Blacks, the prospects for the Auckland game were poor.

On the Sunday morning they flew to Whangarei in the north of New Zealand and took a coach to Waitangi in the Bay of Islands, famous in New Zealand's history as the site where the Maori chieftains signed the country over to Queen Victoria in 1840. On that coach journey Cotton began singing some of the repetition songs he had learned at Loughborough College, and by the time the players disembarked they were in good humour.

Pullin had been to Waitangi with the 1971 Lions and had recommended that England stay there for as long as possible before playing the All Blacks. So the players trained among the citrus trees at KeriKeri and they used their leisure time to the full, both in and out of the water, determined to put the memory of their three recent defeats out of their minds.

Team selection was critical. This time Cotton won the nod over Burton at tight-head prop because Pullin reckoned that New Zealand would not present such a stiff scrummaging test and that Cotton's pace around the field would be valuable. Cotton for Burton and Uttley for Larter were the only alterations from the pack which had beaten South Africa. The half backs, Webster and Old, were the same.

Webster, known as "Sprat", was an inspired choice. He spent time before the game telling everyone that they might as well go out and win "for Piggy's sake" – and even though he was up against the so-called No. 1 scrum-half in the world in Sid Going, Webster played so well that the New Zealand master was outskilled.

The England forwards, well organized and working as a unit, created the sort of pressure which New Zealand normally generated. The back row of Neary, Ripley and Watkins roamed to great effect, while Webster and Old kept driving everyone forward.

It was a windy day on the Eden Park ground and New Zealand led twice in the first half with two tries. Webster, however, had made his mark with a break which gave Squires a first-half try for England and in the second half England put pressure on the All Blacks full back Bob Lendrum. Two mistakes by Lendrum led to England tries, by Stevens and Neary, and although New Zealand mounted a despairing rally in the final minutes Pullin and his team hung on to win 16–10.

"I was always quite confident about taking the All Blacks," says Pullin. "The big match beforehand was against Canterbury and, although we lost that, everyone felt we were playing well. I was optimistic for the Test because they thought we were going to throw it around all afternoon but we always intended to match or beat them up-front."

The England team stayed long in the dressing room, savouring their moment of victory. Sandy Sanders, the manager, was ecstatic. Later, when England went to the match dinner, Jan Webster was allowed to walk up a long flight of stairs ahead of the team, applauded all the way.

That victory, on 15 September 1973, meant that England became the first home country to have beaten New Zealand home and away. Pullin and eight of his players pulled off the unique double of beating South Africa and New Zealand away from home and with little more than a year in between the matches.

England flew out of New Zealand the next day, heading straight for home where the new season had already begun. There was one more match left for England in 1973, against Australia, and they won that as well, 20–3.

For that game, Jan Webster, the little terrier of Auckland, was not required and would play for England just five more times. Steve Smith, who made his debut at scrum-half in 1973, came in against Australia and went on to become England's most capped player in the position, playing 28 times in eleven years.

CHAPTER 11

John Pullin continued supreme in 1974. The Lions were on tour again that year, to South Africa, and Pullin's inclusion looked a certainty. He was even being touted as a possible captain. England, however, began the championship by losing to Scotland at Murrayfield 14–16 when Andy Irvine kicked a penalty for Scotland in the last seconds of the match after Duckham had gone offside. Then Ireland outscored England by four tries to one at Twickenham to win 26–21, and although Pullin equalled Budge Rogers's record of 34 caps for England in that game, mathematically he was overhauled by the Irish captain Willie John McBride whose 56th cap was a world record.

For the French game, England played at the remodelled Parc des Princes for the first time. Like everyone else they had been trekking out to the suburbs for years to play at Stade Colombes, but now the totally enclosed concrete oval in the 16th *arrondissement* of the French capital was their target.

The day before the game, England trained in six inches of snow but they could not have asked for better conditions when the match started and they responded with a 12–12 draw. The match was saved by Duckham with a try following the only threatening back movement, one of the ten he scored in his 36 England appearances.

Duckham was a marvellously gifted player, one of the best I have seen in an England shirt. As a boy he had watched Peter Jackson producing his magic on the wing for Coventry and he was able to follow a similar path himself into the Coventry club, then England, and finally the British Lions.

Initially Duckham and John Spencer played nine games as the England centres before Duckham moved to the wing in 1971, a position he could call his own until he was left out in 1976. He had a great talent and was probably appreciated more in countries such as Wales and New Zealand than anywhere else. England could never claim to have made the fullest use of his skills, and this match in Paris was just one example. Duckham had pace and swerve and supreme ability to finish a movement, but there was no doubt he was neglected by England in an era when Gerald Davies of Wales was showing the way home to every wing in the world.

Paris had been such an unprofitable city for England that a draw was considered good news. England had been beaten 37–12 on their last match at Stade Colombes but they liked the new stadium and have achieved some excellent results there.

The next morning there was considerable confusion at Orly airport, then the chief gateway to Paris, because industrial action in Britain had severely restricted flights by British Airways. Passengers were moved on to other carriers, one of which was Turkish Airlines. The DC10 which Turkish Airlines operated that morning crashed shortly after take-off from Paris for London, killing all on board. Many of those who died, including a large contingent from the Bury St Edmunds club in Suffolk, had come for the match. Later that season England and France played a special match at Twickenham to help the dependants.

The 1974 game against Wales was Duckham's 30th and he was involved in a controversy which lives on – in Wales, anyway – to this day. England won the game 16–12, their first victory against Wales for eleven years, but thousands of Welsh supporters and many Welsh players were convinced that a kick-ahead by the Welsh wing J. J. Williams and subsequent chase for the ball by Williams and the English wings, Duckham and Squires, had ended with the touchdown being gained by Williams. Indeed Duckham told me that evening that he thought Williams had scored. However, the referee, John West of Ireland, considered otherwise.

Ireland became the 1974 champions and McBride, their captain, was appointed captain of the Lions. No one argued with that – it would be his fifth Lions tour – but the fact that Pullin was passed over completely caused more than momentary surprise. In the initial selection England provided two backs. Alan Old and Geoff Evans, and six forwards, Andy Ripley, Tony Neary, Chris Ralston, Mike Burton, Roger Uttley and Fran Cotton.

When the Lions came to play the first Test in Capetown, the team meeting on the morning of the game remains etched in the minds of those players who took part. McBride sat in the team room, a familiar figure to them all with his pipe cradled in his hand, and for what seemed like an eternity said nothing at all. Then he said: "There is no escape, we must go on."

The Lions won the first Test 12–3 and the second 28–9, and everyone knew that the whole tour hinged on the third Test at Port Elizabeth on 13 July.

The mental preparation was enormous. Millar asked the players to concentrate as never before on clearing their minds for the critical third Test. McBride, with a word here, a sentence there, did not let up on his players, whether they were in the Test team or not.

Very few teams have had the unity of those Lions as they headed for the Boet Erasmus stadium in Port Elizabeth, singing "We shall overcome". By the time they arrived at the ground they had switched tunes to their tour battle hymn, "Flower of Scotland". They sang to the final note, then disembarked from their coach.

McBride's last words were aimed straight at the heart. "This is the most important game of our lives," he said. "If we play for another ten years no game will be bigger than this."

Just two England players were part of the Lions Test team, Cotton at prop, Uttley at flanker. There were times on the tour when Ripley and Neary both looked capable of forcing their way into the Test side, but they were not selected.

The tension at the third Test was immense. It was broken, on the field, by one enormous fight when the score was 3–3. Reacting, as they saw it, to the need to demonstrate that they were not intimidated by their opponents, the Lions signalled to all players that they should join in the fracas by using the code number "99" – a call which had also been used in New Zealand in 1971. The South Africans, like the New Zealanders before them, were surprised by the character change. The players were to be widely criticized for their actions. After the fight in Port Elizabeth, the Lions scored their first try when Gordon Brown, the Scottish lock, went over from a short line-out. The final score was 26–9.

The Lions did not make a clean sweep of the series because they drew the final Test 13–13 but each player knew that they had been through a unique experience.

Uttley came home as buoyant as everyone else. Little did he realize that the "Flower of Scotland", which he sang so lustily, would come back to haunt him 16 years later.

CHAPTER 12

In 1975 England handed over the coaching from John Elders to John Burgess. The captaincy was taken away from Pullin as well. Cotton led for three matches, all of which were lost, and the only victory was against Scotland, when Neary was captain.

The one new cap against Ireland, the first opponents, was a lock forward from the Fylde club named Bill Beaumont. A back injury to Uttley gave Beaumont his chance and this unsung beginning to international rugby was to propel on to the England stage one of the key figures in English rugby history.

Beaumont had arrived at the England team via schoolboy experiences at fly-half and full back and then a variety of positions with his only senior club, Fylde, including prop and flanker, before finally settling as a lock forward. Already he had made his mark with Lancashire, and although he did not know it at the time he would follow three Lancashire contemporaries – Uttley, Cotton and Neary – into the England captaincy.

Beaumont's first match was opposite McBride, who had cult-figure status in Ireland by then, but the game went not at all badly for the young man from Fylde. Even so, England were beaten 12–9 after conceding a try from a mistake in front of the posts and Beaumont went straight out of the team. If he felt upset about moving out after one game, he had more than illustrious company because Pullin was dropped as well, giving way to Peter Wheeler of Leicester.

In the summer of 1975 England made their first solo tour of Australia (the 1963 visit was added on to a tour of New Zealand). The selectors clearly thought that the task ahead would not be too exacting, because twelve uncapped players were chosen in the original squad. The plan was to give a chance to raw players who looked on the way up, and it was believed that the environment of a tour, with constant team training, would allow them to develop more quickly than in other circumstances.

Just six of the team which had beaten New Zealand in 1973 were chosen, including Pullin. The most obvious half backs, Alan Old and Steve Smith, were left out in favour of four half backs who had one cap among them. Once on tour England ran into further problems with injuries and started the first Test against Australia in Sydney with five new caps.

Neary, the tour captain, was early on the victim of injured ribs and did not play on the tour again – which meant that Pullin assumed the leadership once more. Neil Bennett, the fly-half, also went off hurt as England stumbled to a 9–16 defeat.

The second Test was just one week later, in Brisbane, and England hurriedly flew out Old as replacement for Bennett and immediately put him into the side. All the reconstruction was quickly forgotten in the first few minutes of a match which became one of the most notorious England have played.

England knew that there were one or two potential hit-men operating in the Australian team and also that the coach, David Brockhoff, who ran a biscuit company, was certain to build the Wallabies up for a match which would clinch the series. There was fighting at the first ruck. There was more fighting in the first line-out, after which Beaumont had to go off to have attention to a cut over his eye. Beaumont was still

62

in the dressing room having stitches inserted when Mike Burton, the prop, joined him. Burton, however, had not come off for attention. He had been sent off by the referee for a late tackle, having already been warned for butting.

Burton remains unique because no other England player has been sent off before or since. The immediate effect was that England had to play most of the Test with 14 men and Beaumont, back on the field with his stitches, had to play in the unfamiliar position of prop as a result. Even with this handicap England led the Aussies 15–9 at half-time, but the pressures of playing a man short began to tell and Australia went on to win 30–21, scoring five tries.

The backlash from the tour was highlighted by the resignation of the coach, John Burgess. There was talk, too, of the Australians not being asked to fulfil the English section of their tour to Britain the next winter.

What particularly grated in the minds of the senior players was the fact that indifferent selection had meant that they could not fulfil themselves. It all seemed such an utter waste of time because the raw material sent on the tour hardly benefited and the experienced players were frustrated. An opportunity to build a hard core for the next few years was wasted.

Another nine years would pass before England toured one of the major countries again. There were expeditions to Argentina and to the USA and Canada but all the players knew that the tours which counted were to South Africa, New Zealand and Australia. England played in all three countries in the eighties ... and came home without a single victory against the national teams.

The 1976 programme began with England being coached by Peter Colston, a former Bristol full back, and with Neary as captain for the five matches which were played. Revenge was gained against Australia by 23–6 but all talk of an England revival was rapidly ended in the championship with a second whitewash. This was complete humiliation, underlined by the largest Welsh win at Twickenham, 21–9, and

England had 86 points scored against them, including 13 tries.

Duckham did not play again after the match with Scotland. Neither did Andy Ripley, a dynamic No. 8 who took up rugby at the age of 19 and turned himself into one of the most admired players of the decade. He was totally unpredictable and his own players rarely knew what to expect from him.

Ripley was also a high-class hurdler – and ran like it on the rugby field, his knees pushing up so that they almost touched his chin – and if his handling had matched all his other abilities he might have had many more caps than the 24 he earned. Ripley played on and on after England discarded him. All his club rugby was with Rosslyn Park, and he captained them, finished his playing time with them at the age of 42, then became club president. He also found time to compete in the "Superstars" television series and in one memorable year was judged third best in the world in this somewhat contrived contest of sporting skills.

Morale was rock-bottom after 1975 and 1976, in which England had lost all but two of eleven international matches, using almost 50 players. So England brought back Sandy Sanders as chairman of selectors, Uttley was made captain, and the progress of Uttley's club, Gosforth, who had won the Cup final at Twickenham for two years, was marked by the selection of three of their players.

The new mixture worked. Uttley wanted everything kept simple, Sanders called on the players to show pride in their play, and off England went into something of a blistering start by beating Scotland by 26–6 (which is still their biggest win over the Scots at Twickenham) and nailing Ireland 4–0 in Dublin.

Thereafter it was downhill. England lost by a single point to France, 3–4, and at Cardiff Alastair Hignell kicked three penalties as England lost 9–14.

For the 1977 Lions tour to New Zealand the England pack was rewarded with the selection of Fran Cotton, Roger

Uttley, Peter Wheeler and Nigel Horton. Neary was chosen as well, but Peter Squires was the only England back to win selection. Uttley did not travel because of a recurrence of back trouble and Horton dropped out injured during the tour and was replaced by Beaumont.

The Lions tour held great significance for England because four of their forwards played against New Zealand in the final Test and Beaumont established himself as a man who could no longer be denied a regular place.

The Lions lost the Test series 3–1. For Beaumont, who played in three Tests, a definite change of status was on the way once he returned to domestic rugby.

CHAPTER 13

Bill Beaumont, like John Pullin, had not been asked to captain a side since he was at school; but within a matter of weeks of returning from New Zealand he was given the leadership of the England side to play against the USA at Twickenham. No caps were awarded for this match because there was a much more rigid attitude then about which opponents merited the award of caps, and the American Eagles did not qualify.

That first step into captaincy was not difficult for Beaumont. His players had easily more ability than the Americans, who represented a fledgling country in rugby terms. The USA Rugby Union had been formed in 1975 and the tour of England was their first in national colours.

The Americans won two of their six matches but were out of their depth against England, who beat them 37–11. It was meant to be an experimental England side yet all but four of the players either had caps or went on to win them.

Once Beaumont and his players moved on to more serious matters, in 1978, again England could master neither France nor Wales; but they did beat Scotland and Ireland – and were left with one match to play that year, against New Zealand.

The All Blacks, under the captaincy of Graham Mourie, a flanker, won all four internationals on this tour and England's selection did little to halt them. England chose John Scott, a promisingly athletic Devonian who had played four games at No. 8, in the second row. They chose a loose-head prop, Barry Nelmes, to play at tight head.

England led twice but New Zealand always looked capable of finding a higher gear, and scored two tries to win 16–6. The match did not go at all well for England, and one of the casualties was Beaumont. He kept his place but was relieved of the captaincy. Uttley took over. Uttley then led in one game before Beaumont was reinstated and played on for a further 16 matches as captain until injury forced him to stop in 1982. England were fortunate that two such fine forwards as Uttley and Beaumont were in contention for the captaincy. Uttley's career was punctuated by injury, while Beaumont had a lengthy run in the side until his sudden departure.

Some of this took place as the All Blacks tour continued; and the controversies on that tour overshadowed the domestic matter of who was the right man to lead England. There was much to be admired about the All Blacks, from their management onwards, but few admired them in Wales.

The Test against Wales was won 13–12, but it was the manner of the New Zealand win which lingers blackly in Welsh memories. Thousands of Welshmen say the final penalty which Brian McKechnie kicked to win the game should never have been awarded. They thought that the referee, Roger Quittenton of England, was fooled by a dive out of a line-out by Andy Haden. Even Haden would admit much later that he was trying to secure a penalty. Quittenton, however, said he ignored that, awarding a penalty because Wales had obstructed in the line-out. This was a bitter pill for Welsh rugby to swallow – they were still in the glorious seventies when victories came regularly and easily – and contributed to a sour atmosphere at most of the All Blacks games in Wales.

The penultimate match was at Bridgend, home club of J. P. R. Williams, then well on his way to becoming the most capped full back for Wales, with 55 appearances. In muddy and wet conditions Williams was trapped on the ground under a ruck and an All Blacks forward trod on his face. The wound required stitches and the scar can be seen to this day.

What was clear about this incident in the mud at the Brewery Field was that Williams, a high-profile player renowned for his combative play from full back, had suffered a dreadful injury when he was unable to move or defend himself. Television highlighted what had happened but the All Blacks management, so admired in every other way, said they had not seen it – and declined an invitation to watch the video tape of the incident.

Mourie, the All Blacks captain and open-side flanker, was an outstanding player, even by New Zealand's high standards. He was determined to be fitter than anyone else he played with or against, and had enough experience of winning matches in the final minutes to justify his beliefs. He did not miss a trick in public relations, either. He was painstaking in his responsibilities to the media, which he regarded as a full part of his job as captain of New Zealand. He represented a new breed in captaincy and set a pattern of behaviour which others followed. The All Blacks lost one match on the tour, to Munster at Limerick, and of their three close games one was particularly significant – the 9–6 score by which they beat the North of England, led by Beaumont, at Birkenhead Park. Beaumont and the North players were to remember the lessons of that day.

*　*　*

The tour had been watched closely by Will Carling, who had turned 13 four days before the New Zealanders won their last game against the Barbarians at Cardiff. Carling remembers how impressed he was with Mourie – how he led the team and the things he said. As the second son in an army family Carling was becoming used to their frequent changes of home – the Carlings had 24 different addresses during his father's army service – but the one permanent feature of his early life was his love of rugby.

68

Carling's first schooling was at the Montgomery County Infants' School in Colchester. He remembers being a bit of a bully there and embarrassing others with his behaviour, but his time at a school which played soccer passed normally. Already he was experimenting with garden rugby, scoring tries for imaginary teams in front of imaginary crowds, or sometimes he would play a game on his own in his bedroom, scoring tries there as well.

By the time he was seven, Carling was being assessed as "very agile" by his school class teacher, a Mrs Goodridge, who also noted that he was "very neat" in written work and that he produced interesting accounts and imaginative stories. He was described as a thoughtful little boy, a good worker.

After three years in Colchester a fresh posting for his father provided Carling – and his brother – with a change of school. He went to Terra Nova in Cheshire, a boarding school, and remained there until he was 13. His parents took him to the school and watched him walk up the stairs, never looking back.

At the end of Carling's first term at Terra Nova the headmaster, Andrew Keith, was moved to comment: "Outside the classroom William has found himself in hot water a little too often. He needs to be a little more thoughtful and considerate. He has had great success on the rugger field, displaying a nice balance between toughness and skill." The following April Carling was reminded that he must be conscious of "the needs of others and considerate of their feelings" yet within a couple of months the same teacher saw "less of his bullishness and more consideration and leadership".

Carling played all kinds of rugby at Terra Nova, sometimes nine- or ten-a-side, but never played the game of mini-rugby which thousands use as their introduction to the sport now. He captained various teams in the green and white hooped shirts of Terra Nova. Sometimes he played fly-half in his own age group or sometimes he moved up a couple of age bands and played on the wing in the same side as his brother. His captaincy was described as "splendid" by the headmaster. And when in 1979 Carling completed his time at Terra Nova, to move on to Sedbergh, having won the shooting cup with an average of 96.8 in 20 competitive shoots over a three-year period, the headmaster commented: "He has dominated much of Terra Nova life for a fair amount of time and much of our sporting and artistic success is due to him. I hope that William can make the adjustment from being master of all he surveys to being just another lowly new boy with the right degree of humour and humility."

CHAPTER 14

Bill Beaumont's style of leadership was open and honest. He played with utter dedication to his team and it was always obvious that he would compete until he dropped. He was not a natural athlete nor a graceful mover, but at the front of the line-out or leading his men forward with the ball in his hands he was like granite on the move.

Beaumont also had the happy knack of being in harmony with the England supporters. They felt he was playing for them just as much as he was playing for the team. He had time for the fans, a quick word here and there, always smiling. When Beaumont pounded those lonely miles in training around Chorley, the headquarters of the family textile firm, it was if the loyalty of all those fans was driving him on.

If Uttley had maintained anything like normal fitness he might have locked Beaumont out of the captaincy. Beaumont won 34 caps against 23 by Uttley. Beaumont's caps came over an eight-season period, the same span as Uttley; but neither has any regrets about what happened to them in the playing of the game or of subsequent events.

That Beaumont came to the England captaincy by accident is not unusual. Many others have climbed in on the back of an injured player. In a sense that was how Carling was propelled forward, while Beaumont's own period as captain was also to end as a result of injury.

Beaumont's first important match in 1979 was against France, the reigning champions. Beaumont played exceptionally well in England's 7–6 win at Twickenham but everything else was disappointment. There was a draw with Scotland and bad defeats in Dublin and in Cardiff.

The England side which finished the championship contained only six players who were going to be automatic choices in the Grand Slam team the following year. However, two overseas experiences went into shaping that England squad and greatly influenced the way they played.

That autumn, England took a tour party to the Far East under the management of Budge Rogers, the Bedford flanker who was the new chairman of selectors; Mike Davis went as coach. Davis had had a spectacular run as coach to the England Schools' teams and leapfrogged to the senior job without coaching anyone else. He had long been regarded as an astute selector; now he was to be tested on another front.

The tour went to Japan, Fiji and Tonga, and England won all their seven matches – even if the opening international against Japan in Osaka was not won until injury time when Peter Squires, who scored the late try to beat Fiji in 1973, did so again.

The players were impressed by Davis and his methods. They liked his organization and training sessions and felt that a framework was being constructed from which a promising England team could emerge. Beaumont was a tower of strength throughout the tour. Equally Davis was learning day by day about the men who were going to be vital to him in the coming months.

The other tour which had a considerable bearing on English rugby later in that close season was by North West Counties, who went on a pioneering trip to South Africa and took with them a powerful collection of England backs. That tour also marked the return to regular play of Fran Cotton who had been out for a year with a torn achilles tendon.

The North West took on some tough fixtures against Western Province, Orange Free State, Natal and Northern

Transvaal. Of the two wins, that over Northern Transvaal, the South African provincial champions, was the most rewarding. Cotton proved his form after his return from injury, and the backs – Steve Smith and John Horton, Mike Slemen, Tony Bond and John Carleton – were impressive also.

By the autumn of 1979 there was an encouraging spread of skill and experience in the England ranks – particularly pleasing since New Zealand had to be faced for the second time in a year. The feeling was that England had learned lessons from the 1978 match against New Zealand and these could be put into practice in the 1979 game.

One week before the England–New Zealand game, the North of England faced the All Blacks at the Otley club in Yorkshire. There was so much strength in Northern rugby at the time, so much self-belief engendered by the coach, Des Seabrook, that anyone deeply involved with their preparations knew they would do well.

Seabrook set a rigid training pattern, using a couple of Yorkshire clubs as his base camps, and once a week in the month preceding the game the men of the North concentrated on making every single factor of their team-play as smooth as possible. The aim was to tie down the All Blacks, again led by Graham Mourie, and stifle their chances.

The New Zealanders began their tour against London at Twickenham and, scraping through 21–18, were surprised by the quality of the players and the strength of the London side's organization for what was meant to be an easy-paced start. Then Mourie's men hit their stride, and by the time they arrived at Otley for the match on 17 November they had dismissed Scotland 20–6 and beaten the Midlands at Leicester by 33–6, their biggest win of the tour. Otley represented the eighth game of an eleven-match tour.

Beaumont was made captain of the North. Uttley, who had recovered from the shock of being chosen captain of England against Ireland the previous February – a match he missed through injury – then dropped altogether, was chosen

73

at tight flanker. In each row of the pack there were committed men. The back row was particularly impressive because Tony Neary and Peter Dixon were there with Uttley. To complete that section of the side which would be needed to play a ten-man game, Steve Smith and Alan Old were selected at half back.

The New Zealanders played their full Test side. As they took the field they must have realized they were in for a grim day. The ground was jammed with thousands of spectators, some of them hanging on to the trees at the far end of the pitch from the dressing rooms. The wind blew hard and it was wet – conditions which New Zealanders are well used to – but the elements of the day ensured that the North players had a lot going for them.

The All Blacks had the wind first but it was no friend to them. The North forwards took them on with a mixture of ferocity and cunning, just as their game-plan had dictated. It was wonderful stuff, fuelled from within but encouraged every inch of the way by the crowd.

At half-time the North led by a try and a penalty, 7–0. Early in the second half the All Blacks cut back the deficit, but two tries from Tony Bond, the Sale centre who relished his battering-ram role, took the game away from the tourists. Eventually the North scored four tries, each one of them a savage blow to those New Zealanders. The final score was 21–9, one of the most convincing victories in the long history of English provincial teams against touring sides.

There were six players in the North side – Beaumont, Dixon, Uttley, Neary, Cotton and Smith – who either had or would captain England, and although the euphoria that night was intense and spread into every part of Otley and the North, the senior men realized that some of them would have to be ready to face the All Blacks again at Twickenham in the Test the following Saturday.

The morning after the North victory the England squad trained at Leicester. Budge Rogers, the chairman of selectors, told the players what the team would be and then made the public announcement. Just seven of the North side progressed from Otley to Twickenham. There was no room for Uttley, nor for Old. Instead the selectors went for the half-back pairing of Smith and a new cap, Les Cusworth, a Yorkshireman who was fly-half for Leicester, having played previously for Wakefield and Moseley. At flanker, Mike Rafter of Bristol, known as "Rafter the Grafter", displaced Uttley.

Apparently the selectors did not want to base their judgement of the England side solely on what the North had done. They felt that the North players might not be able to peak against the All Blacks twice in eight days. They never knew, because they did not give them the chance.

The worst thing to do to a New Zealand team is to beat them; the second worst is to make their chances easier in the next big game. So England took the field lacking some of the strengths available to them, and were duly beaten 10–9. At one stage New Zealand led 10–3, which was a fairer reflection of the gap between the teams.

Beaumont was as disappointed as anyone else in and around the squad. He was not to know that it was his last match against New Zealand – and the great prize of a victory over the All Blacks had been missed.

That was how 1979 ended for England. It was of no significance at the time that an England "B" team was beaten 25–9 by France at a match in Brussels. The England team included a lock forward named Paul Ackford, then a student at Cambridge University. He made little impact.

CHAPTER 15

On 5 January 1980 England beat the Rest in a trial at Twickenham. The one player who used this as a definite stepping-stone was Phil Blakeway, a prop from Gloucester. Blakeway had the reputation as a strongman and had been on the tour to Australia in 1975. In between that and his first selection for the England side he had survived a broken neck and had returned to play more solidly than anyone had anticipated.

Blakeway caused a sensation in the trial with his work against the England front row and it was an inspired piece of selection to choose him on the evidence of that match. Blakeway was as proud as any player I have known to wear the England shirt and had a devotion to duty so strong it could almost be touched. England chose him to play at tight-head prop and he responded by saying he would not be shifted by the opposition. It was an agreeable arrangement.

So the front row formed – Blakeway, Peter Wheeler at hooker, winning his 21st cap, and Fran Cotton at loose-head prop, winning his 27th cap. Beaumont, winning his 23rd cap, was at lock with Nigel Horton, winning his 20th and final cap, alongside.

On the flanks were Uttley, winning his 20th cap, and Neary, in for his 40th appearance, while at No. 8 was John Scott, winning his eleventh cap. Nobody could argue with that combination, blessed with talent and a colossal sense of motivation to achieve something. All the players involved in 1980 believed in each other and thought the selections were right.

The backs were reshuffled. John Horton was reinstated at fly-half after a year out of favour. The wings were the best in Britain, John Carleton and Mike Slemen, and the centres contrasted Bond's urgency and aggression with Nick Preston's smooth running. Behind at full back was the goal kicker supreme, Dusty Hare.

The team looked very solid on paper but Ireland, their first opponents, were heading to Twickenham as favourites for the championship. They had had a benchmark tour of Australia the previous summer, winning both Tests, and a goal-kicker feared throughout the world in fly-half Ollie Campbell.

Campbell was soon in business, kicking three penalties in the first quarter of the game against one by Hare. This went totally against Beaumont's planning that the England forwards should dominate and not give Campbell the chance to kick goals.

However, by half-time England had the match running their way with tries from scrum-half Steve Smith and Slemen, and in the second half Scott added a third to point England towards an eventual 24–9 win. There was one serious loss that January afternoon: Tony Bond broke a leg after an hour's play and had to be replaced by Clive Woodward of Leicester.

Woodward stayed for the rest of the season. Maurice Colclough came back after injury to displace Horton and, as he spoke French, it meant that there was at least one interpreter in the pack for the visit to Paris.

Despite the margin against Ireland the familiar old story appeared to be facing England against France. They had not won in Paris since 1964 and when Mr Flamboyance himself, French captain Jean-Pierre Rives, scored a try in the second minute the hearts of the English supporters sank.

Beaumont, however, was unconvinced. He reminded his

forwards that they had come to do a job. The England pack dug in and set up command. Blakeway, propping opposite a converted No. 8, had a field day, while Cotton was busy on the other side of the front row dispensing his own brand of power and authority. England even dropped a goal from possession won by a seven-man pack when Uttley was off having attention to a cut.

England's two tries both came in the first half, the first by Preston, the second by Carleton. Horton dropped a second goal and Hare kicked a penalty, and even though France rallied and fought to the end, the result was 17–13 in England's favour.

That evening, in the bars around the Parc des Princes, the England supporters celebrated their victory. Great choruses of the national anthem went up to the sky, while the England players, exhausted and elated at the same time, rejoiced – they had broken one of the great barriers. Suddenly the words "Grand Slam" were in the air.

The next two weeks produced a state of tension which may never have been equalled before an England–Wales match at Twickenham. Here were two unbeaten sides (Wales had also beaten France) on collision course and the Grand Slam, which Wales had won three times in the seventies, was an option to both teams.

There had been calls for the Welsh selectors not to choose Paul Ringer at flanker because of an allegation that he had overstepped the mark against France and that television had shown him to be in the wrong. Whatever, Ringer was chosen to play against England – an added source of tension.

A third factor to be considered was the rivalry between Cotton and Graham Price, the Welsh tight-head prop. Stories went this way and that about what they were going to do to one another when battle commenced, and even if they did not have much foundation they persisted. Scott, the England No. 8, who did not mind telling anyone how good he thought he was, actually played for Cardiff and so would be facing three men from his own club.

By the time England and Wales took the pitch, the pressure-cooker atmosphere was all too obvious. The build-up had taken the attitudes of players on both sides beyond previous limits and transmitted itself to the huge crowd as well. It was bear-pit time, Twickenham style.

The referee was David Burnett of Ireland. It was his second England–Wales match, and he must have realized from the kick-off that it was going to present him with a difficult afternoon. The boots and fists of desperately anxious men went in from the start. Cynical fouls proliferated.

The terror was now of tidal-wave proportions but bad blood was rising so fast that Burnett called together the two captains, Beaumont and Jeff Squire of Pontypool, to warn them that the next act of foul play would lead to a sending-off. Both captains took the message back to their players.

Within minutes the sending-off which Burnett had threatened did take place. Horton had kicked ahead when he was tackled late by Ringer, already labelled a brigand in the pre-game skirmishing. Ringer departed, and although none of the players thought later that he had done anything particularly wrong, they did feel that his timing was not of the finest.

In fact the sending-off made little difference to the general tone of the contest. The warfare continued, with nobody wanting to back down, and Wales responded solidly to the need to lift their game now that they were left with only 14 men. To have beaten England at Twickenham with just 14 players! It nearly happened, too.

Hare kicked the penalty which was awarded when Ringer was dismissed. Wales countered immediately with a try from Squire who pounced on a ball which came out of the side of a wheeling scrum.

England lost Uttley with a split nose at half-time – Rafter took his place – and this most gruelling of contests stayed on the same score until 15 minutes from time when Hare kicked his second penalty. Next, with three minutes left, Wales took the lead again with a second try. Phillips, the Welsh hooker, charged down a kick by Smith near half-way and set off for the England line, turning the ball to his supporting wing, Elgan Rees, who raced on to score. Wales led 8–6.

England piled back, attacking down the west touchline, and forced a penalty, wide out, which they knew was their final chance. Hare was given the ball, facing fame or failure. He struck his kick perfectly and the ball sailed off in the mist, right on target, and England had won by one point, 9–8.

Looked at objectively, England were now one victory short of the Grand Slam, but rugby was the loser that February day. The players who used the boot and the fist indiscriminately were losers and those who retaliated were losers. Those who had inflamed passions beforehand were losers and those who would not condemn it afterwards were losers as well. Rugby would have died on its feet long ago if what happened in and around that day became the norm. The bitterness experienced in that match has not repeated itself, not over such a long period as virtually an entire contest, and the players who were involved that day have put it into context in their own minds and learned from it.

Everyone had to look forward from that game, because there was not much pleasure in looking back, and Wales reacted by criticizing their players and warning that such behaviour must not be repeated. Wales went on to beat Scotland 17–6, then lost 21–7 to Ireland. England, meanwhile, had a full month between beating Wales and going to Murrayfield for the most important match of their lives. The side which had started against Wales was repeated against Scotland, who were led from full back by Andy Irvine, and were playing one of their most profitable half-back partnerships, John Rutherford and Roy Laidlaw, for the third time.

During this championship campaign England trained on Monday evenings at the Stourbridge club in Worcestershire. By the time they began preparations for the Scotland game, the crowds at Stourbridge to see them work out would not have disgraced a Football League attendance in one of the lower divisions. Stourbridge had to use a commissionaire on the door of the clubhouse to sift out who was who. When their training was over the players dined royally from large cuts of roast beef. It was at Stourbridge that the last part of the Grand Slam journey was planned and perfected.

Few England teams had travelled to Murrayfield as confidently as this one – and with justification. Sale provided two players to the England team in the shape of Cotton and Smith and Leicester four. The Leicester player providing real impact was Woodward, at centre, whose clever running with instinctive changes of pace and direction paved the way for two quick tries by Carleton and Slemen. The foundation was laid.

England were ahead 19–3 at half-time. Early in the second half a surging move involving most of the team put Smith across for another try. Carleton then completed his hat trick, the first by an England player since 1924 (also a Grand Slam year), and although Scotland were fully in the match in the final stages, the verdict deservedly went to the ambitious England side by 30–18.

Uttley did not play for England again after that match. Neither did Neary, who had established a new record of 43 appearances. It would be eleven years and the end of another successful Grand Slam for England before Neary's total would be equalled, by Rory Underwood. Beaumont was the first England captain since Eric Evans in 1957 to lead a Grand Slam side – he had another and rapid reward because, fewer than 48 hours after winning at Murrayfield, he was named captain of the Lions tour to South Africa.

CHAPTER 16

No English player had captained the Lions since Doug Prentice of Leicester – who later became secretary of the Rugby Football Union – headed the 1930 tour of New Zealand and Australia. Beaumont's Lions were under the management of two former Irish players, Syd Millar and Noel Murphy, the coach, and selection was hampered by the fact that a number of leading players were unavailable. The tour cried out for flankers with pace and experience but neither Fergus Slattery of Ireland nor Tony Neary of England, the top two of the time, was available.

Seven of Beaumont's Grand Slam team were chosen with him but some were to fall by the wayside long before the 18-match tour was completed. Blakeway departed with a rib injury after the second game. In the sixth match Cotton became a casualty of a different kind when he left the field with chest pains, and for a time during his hospital treatment afterwards there were suggestions that he had suffered a heart attack. This proved not to be the case.

Another England player who left the tour early, this time for family reasons, was Mike Slemen, the wing, and it did not take the Lions long to realize that the mission was going to be all the more strenuous as a result. By the time of the second Test in mid-June, seven Lions had already gone home. Another soon followed, which meant that eight players had to fly out to join the Lions. One of the replacements was Steve Smith, the England scrum-half, who created history by actually not playing a single game in the short time he spent in South Africa.

This was the last Lions tour to South Africa and the series was won by the Springboks as they took the first three Tests 26–22, 26–19 and 12–10. The Lions suffered a piece of real misfortune in the third Test, played in wind and rain at Port Elizabeth, because it was decided by an accident. Clive Woodward trickled a clearance kick into touch and the Springboks took a quick throw, with the Lions defence way out of contact, and scored the decisive try. This left Beaumont and his men with the task of salvaging their pride in the fourth Test at Pretoria.

Beaumont knew that defeat in the final Test would make him the first captain of the Lions this century to suffer a complete whitewash in South Africa; but that was not the only reason why he went from man to man in his squad, reminding each one that they were a better side than their record suggested and that they could pull off a final win before leaving for home. Beaumont had his wish; even though the Lions were behind 7–13 in the second half, they recovered to score two tries and win the game 17–13. It left a question hanging over the Lions of how good they might have been if their plans had not been affected so drastically by injuries.

Beaumont's place as England captain was nonetheless assured for 1981 but already his Grand Slam squad was breaking up. Neary and Uttley, the flankers, were the first to go, Neary because of injury and business commitments, Uttley because of a recurrence of a back injury.

Cotton, the seemingly indestructible anchor-man of so many front rows in the seventies, quit during the first match of the 1981 championship against Wales in Cardiff and did not play again. It was in that match, too, that England scored 19 points with a try and five penalties – all the points coming via full back Dusty Hare – but were still beaten 21–19.

Wales were in their centenary season and knew that the

England pack would threaten them all the way through. However, a disorganized force, which England became when Cotton departed, took time to regroup. Even so, Wales did not win until injury time when Woodward was inveigled into going offside at a scrum close to the England line, and Steve Fenwick won the match with his fourth penalty.

Two wins followed for England. With Huw Davies, a wily footballer from Stourbridge and Cambridge University, appearing at fly-half for the first time, they beat Scotland 23–17. Then England defeated Ireland 10–6 in Dublin and introduced the richly talented Marcus Rose, another Cambridge man, at full back. Two weeks later Rose kicked four second-half penalties at Twickenham ... but France still won 16–12.

In summer 1981 England set off for Argentina at last; there were no threats from guerrilla groups or anyone else, apart from the Pumas who gave England two demanding Tests in Buenos Aires. For the first time England awarded caps against Argentina, and Tony Swift, a wing then with Swansea and later with Bath, plus two Gloucester forwards, Steve Mills and John Fidler, made their first appearances.

Davies now looked to be set for something of a run at fly-half (eventually he played both at centre and full-back for England as well) and made a classic outside break to score one of the three tries against Argentina in the first Test. Yet England only saved that match 19–19 and won the second 12–6, playing exactly the same side. Davies also scored England's one try in that game. England came home knowing that more Southern Hemisphere opposition was on the agenda because Australia were to make a full tour of the British Isles and Ireland – and England were their final Test opponents at Twickenham on 2 January 1982.

In November 1981 an England "B" match took place against France at Bristol and had a considerable bearing on future events. Nigel Melville led the "B" team. Peter Winterbottom and Mike Teague, who were to be in the Grand Slam team ten years later, also played. England won the match, too, 20–10.

Winterbottom won immediate reward because he was the only player to progress from the Bristol match straight into the team against Australia, so winning his first cap. This hard Yorkshire flanker was then 21 and would become a player much respected by the England selectors, admired by his opponents and unstinting in his effort for the team. Only injuries, and the occasional failure by the selectors to choose him, prevented Winterbottom from becoming England's most capped forward in quick time.

Winterbottom almost had a try in his first match for England, because he came close to a touchdown after charging down an Australian kick. Otherwise the match was noteworthy not so much for Winterbottom's first appearance but for the anchor work of Maurice Colclough in the second row and the totally unexpected appearance at half-time of a young lady called Erica Roe.

Beaumont had gathered his team together and was trying to instil into the players the need to concentrate and hold the lead against this highly mobile Australian side when it became clear to him that concentration was the last thing on their minds. Miss Roe had appeared at the south end of the ground and attracted attention on three counts – she was on the pitch, she had an ample bosom and she was topless. She created a considerable diversion and earned a place in Twickenham legend. England were undistracted. The score was 15–11 and given that Australia had players like Simon Poidevin, Mark Loane, Greg Cornelsen, John Hipwell, Mark Ella and Brendan Moon, it represented a profitable day for England.

The 1982 championship began for England at Murrayfield, where Scotland gained a draw 9–9 in injury time with a penalty from within his own half by their captain Andy Irvine. It was not much of a game, with two evenly matched teams cancelling each other out and producing one of the regular series of draws between the two countries. Beaumont reflected that a draw and an away point was better than losing at the start of the championship, and looked ahead to better things.

Beaumont's next important assignment was to play for Lancashire, in their centenary year, in the county championship final against North Midlands at Moseley. In the 37th minute he sustained a blow to the back of his head and decided to withdraw. So it was there, at the Reddings, that Beaumont brought the curtain down on his active rugby career. He did not play again.

The following Monday, with the drizzle settling in at Stourbridge rugby club, Beaumont was at one end of the pitch and the England squad was at the other. He took a last look at them, pulled the collar of his dark-blue overcoat up around his neck, lit a cigarette and walked off. Words of comfort came from strangers ... "Bad luck, Bill", "You'll be back, Bill", "Tough, Bill". Only he knew how tough it was. After 21 games as captain of England and 33 consecutive appearances he had gone.

Beaumont was diagnosed as suffering from concussion and this prevented him from playing against Ireland. It had been hoped that he would be fully recovered in time for the game against France, but the medical advice was that Beaumont had simply taken too much to run the risk of receiving any more blows to the head.

Not until 1991, with Carling's team, was the ghost of Beaumont's 1980 Grand Slam side laid to rest. In that period Beaumont would become a household name through his regular appearances as another sort of team captain on the BBC television programme, "A Question of Sport".

Because he wrote a book about his experiences in rugby and took the proceeds rather than donating them to charity or a rugby club Beaumont was declared a professional by the Rugby Football Union. So, for the same reason, was Fran Cotton. as was Mike Davis, the Grand Slam coach, although his book was never published. They were penalized by the International Board bye-laws of the day and all three have since been reinstated. All have returned to play a full part in rugby, Beaumont and Cotton with the Northern division and its clubs and counties, Davis as coaching director of Harlequins.

1 Defiance personified: Wavell Wakefield, shown here wearing the Harlequins shirt and the knee-length pocketless shorts of his day, was one of the most innovatory and influential players in English rugby in the twenties, and later became an administrator and leading figure on the committees of the Rugby Football Union and Harlequins. A former pupil of Sedbergh school, Wakefield went on to captain England – a tradition continued by John Spencer and Will Carling.

2 Eric Evans, one of the most emotive of England captains, ready for play. A rampaging hooker, Evans led from the front, always eager to show his men the way. His greatest triumph was to captain the 1957 England team to victory in the Grand Slam. He died shortly before the 1991 England team achieved the same feat.

3 The kicking style of Bob Hillier gives away the period. His toe-end kicking is unlikely to be used by any contemporary international players. Indeed, while Hillier was playing in the sixties and seventies the supremely gifted Barry John of Wales was producing equally satisfactory results with his side-of-the-foot technique, since copied and modified by many. Even so, Hillier did produce results and was feared by everyone he played against. His span with England was from 1968 to 1972 and he led the side which beat South Africa at Twickenham in 1969.

4 John Pullin, the England hooker, in play against Wales at Cardiff in 1975 under the watchful eye of prop Fran Cotton. During his long England career Pullin has never won in Wales, but there were other compensations for Pullin: he scored the try which gave England their 11–8 victory over South Africa at Twickenham on 20 December 1989 on the last Springboks tour of Britain. He later led England to victory over South Africa in Johannesburg and over New Zealand in Auckland.

5 In the long history of English rugby few kicks were as critical as this one. Dusty Hare, the farmer from Newark, put it over from in front of the West stand at Twickenham in 1980 to give England a 9–8 victory over Wales and leave them with one match to play, and win, against Scotland for a Grand Slam – in which Hare kicked a further three penalties for England.

6 Peter Wheeler, England's hooker and captain, and Murray Mexted, the New Zealand No. 8, meet after the 1983 Twickenham game when England recorded their first home win over the All Blacks since 1936.

7 A typical charge by Bill Beaumont – here with Uttley in support – during his time in the England second row which began in 1975 and continued until he was forced to retire from injury in 1982 after winning 34 caps. His captaincy included the leadership of the 1980 Grand Slam side and, later that year, the British Lions tour of South Africa.

8 The fast hands of Nigel Melville marked him down as a player to watch from his schooldays and despite a succession of injuries he gradually made his way to the top, culminating in his first appearance for England in 1984, against Australia at Twickenham, when he was also made captain of the side. Melville, pictured here against Wales in 1985, continued to play for England until 1988 when severe leg and ankle injuries finally ended his international career. After a lengthy recovery period Melville has re-emerged with his home club, Otley, at scrum-half.

9 Will Carling (left) and Nigel Melville played in the same England side on only four occasions – all in 1988 – until Melville's captaincy was cut short and Carling took over. Both men made their first impression in the Yorkshire Schools team.

10 Will Carling addresses the England squad – with Jeremy Guscott, Richard Hill, Brian Moore and Paul Ackford in attendance. Carling had to learn his captaincy on the run and became decidedly more assertive after the 1990 defeat to Scotland when the leadership of the side was not as obvious as it might have been. He had another low point with the defeat to Argentina later that year, but the winter of 1990–1 saw England unbeaten.

11 Will Carling scores the first try of the game against Wales at Twickenham in 1990 – a match which ended in a record 34–6 defeat for Wales. Carling took on the Welsh defence in a powerful surge for the North-West corner of the ground. Mark Titley ended up outside the touchline after being wrong-footed and Andy Allen, the Newbridge forward, arrives too late to stop Carling but is clearly wound up with frustration at doing so. Carling's bludgeoning run to score helped obliterate the memory of the previous year's defeat against Wales at Cardiff.

12 Mike Teague is congratulated by Brian Moore after scoring England's only try against Wales in the opening match of the 1991 championship at Cardiff.

13 Simon Hodgkinson, the England full back, contributed a record 60 points in the 1991 Grand Slam campaign, six more than the previous record, scored by Jean Patrick Lescarboura for France in 1984. Hodgkinson's 18 penalties in the 1991 championship were also a record. He began against Wales at Cardiff with seven penalties, a record of any player in a single game.

14 Rory Underwood has been playing for England since 1984 and is now his country's most capped wing. At the same time he has been putting in quality performances for Leicester and been one of the spearheads for their adventurous style of play. Here he is in play for Leicester in harness with Paul Dodge, the England centre who retired in 1991, against Harlequins' Jamie Salmon and Adrian Thompson.

15 Fitness is a continuing worry for Chris Oti, who made his debut for England on the left wing in 1988. Since then he has not been able to play a full season because of injuries and had to pull out of the 1989 British Lions' tour of Australia before the Test series began. The England management have kept faith with Oti, even when he has had next to no match practice, in what is a deliberate attempt to encourage him. He is regarded as one of the most difficult wings in the world to stop. Here he duels with Ieuan Evans of Wales, one of his outstanding rivals.

16 A familiar scene from England's 1991 campaign – Will Carling in possession, Dean Richards in support. In 1990 England played an expansive midfield game but still lost at the final Grand Slam hurdle against Scotland. Richards missed the 1990 championship but on his return in 1991 England changed tactics to accommodate the huge talent of the Leicester No. 8. Richards became a vital force in midfield, either to spearhead drives or support the backs.

17 Jeremy Guscott in play for England against France in 1990. England won 26–7 in a performance of quality and perception the like of which has rarely been seen in an away match. Guscott scored one of the three England tries in Paris, kicking on and regathering the ball after it had rebounded from Will Carling.

18 Rob Andrew's first match for England in 1985 was marked by his beginning an attack from his own half in the opening seconds against Romania at Twickenham. Yorkshire-born Andrew, now a chartered surveyor in London, became England's most capped fly-half in 1991. He played in all England's championship matches in 1985, 1986, 1989, 1990 and 1991, and was captain of Wasps when they won the Courage Clubs' Championship in 1990. By the time he completed his 36th game against France in 1991 he had amassed 132 points from 28 penalties, nine conversions, and ten dropped goals.

19 Andrew in the 1991 Ireland game with Hill in support.

20 Richard Hill has no support in sight as he is stopped by Daniel Charvet, with Philippe Sella in close attendance, during the 1990 France–England match. Blustery conditions were just one of the factors to be overcome that day on the way to England's 26–7 victory.

21 The England front row of 1991, Jeff Probyn, Brian Moore and Jason Leonard, in formation during the match against Ireland in Dublin in 1991. Probyn and Moore have been in harness since 1988; Leonard was 21 when he was chosen for the 1990 tour of Argentina. By the time of the championship the trio were the undisputed first choice. Jeff Probyn is a director of a company which produces reproduction furniture and is an expert yachtsman. He matured slowly into an England prop; he was first capped in 1988, at the age of 31, having played for five different clubs, three different counties, London and England "B".

22 & 23 International hookers are famed for having plenty to say on all topics involving rugby and Brian Moore is no exception. He has a fast mind and quick tongue, and can debate rugby with clarity and conviction for hours. When the mood took him, Moore was able to don a tutu and join a ballet class *en pointe,* as fig. 23 shows. His determination to be the best in his position is reflected in his having achieved 22 caps in succession for England from his first appearance in 1987. He was born in 1962 and is a law graduate from Nottingham University. He played for Nottingham until 1990 when he moved to London to work in corporate finance and joined Harlequins.

Captions to pictures 24–40 are on pp 123–6

4

5

6

7

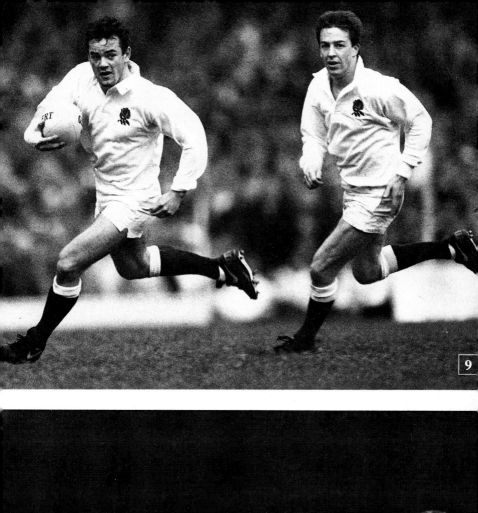

17

21

22

23

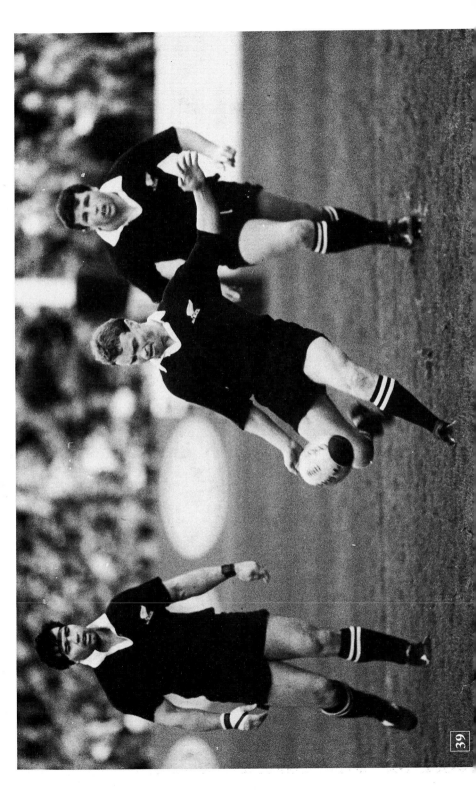

39

24 England had their sights on Jason Leonard long before he made his debut against Argentina in Buenos Aires in 1990. Leonard was chosen for England Colts when he was playing for the Barking club in Essex. Next he moved to Saracens and while he was there he played at loose-head prop because another player was getting married – and has remained in this position since. A carpenter and joiner, Leonard joined Harlequins after the tour to Argentina.

25 Paul Ackford is proof that international recognition is not just for the young. England earmarked him as long ago as 1979, when he was selected for the "B" team, but he was not capped until 1988 at the age of 30. Ackford responded in full measure, rapidly becoming a key member of the England pack, a front jumper in the line-out respected around the world, and a British Lion – all in the space of eight months. An inspector with the Met. Police, he owes much to the vision of Dick Best, the Harlequins and London coach, who believed Ackford had all the assets to reach the top of the game. His partnership with Wade Dooley in the England second row dovetails two contrasting talents and has earned them fame to equal that of Currie and Marques in the fifties.

26 When Wade Dooley eventually stops playing international rugby he can only wonder what might have been if England had picked him up at a younger age. Even starting as late as 27 he became England's most capped second-row forward within six years, passing the total of 34 established by Bill Beaumont. Back in 1985, when he made his first appearance against Romania at Twickenham, Dooley realized he was off the pace for international rugby and set to work to improve his fitness – so much so that his police uniform had to be adjusted to his new, trimmer shape. One of the most important milestones in his career was his elevation to the British Lions Test pack in Australia in 1989 over the head of Robert Norster of Wales, one of the line-out forwards he respects most. Born in Warrington in 1957, Dooley stands 6ft. 8ins. and weighs nearly 18st.

Captions to pictures 1–23 are on pp 87–90

27 Everyone knew the match was already settled when Mike Teague scored a try for England against Ireland in Dublin in 1991 but it was received with as much enthusiasm as that by Rory Underwood which turned the game and sent England on to victory by 16–7. Teague had played at No. 8 in the 1990 championship but reverted to blindside flanker the next season when Dean Richards returned. It was a harmonious arrangement because Richards and Teague were able to continue the powerful playing relationship they forged with the British Lions in Australia in 1989. Teague scored two out of England's five tries in the 1991 championship.

28 By the time he joined the 1991 Grand Slam team, Peter Winterbottom (centre) had been an England player for nine years. He played his early rugby at flanker with Headingley and Yorkshire, gaining valuable experience with club teams in South Africa and New Zealand. A move to London to play for Harlequins led to his taking a job in the City. He captained Quins in their 1991 Pilkington Cup final win over Northampton.

29 Dean Richards surveys the scene before engaging in another scrum for England.

30 Geoff Cooke was appointed in the autumn of 1987 as England's manager for the 1991 World Cup and his job is confirmed until the end of the 1992 five nations' championship. Cooke is chief executive of the British Institute of Sports Coaches, based in Leeds. He had a long association with rugby in Yorkshire and the North before taking the England job. He heads a three-man management team with coach Roger Uttley and John Elliott but also takes advice from a wide range of senior English players and coaches.

31 Roger Uttley is the eighth England rugby coach in succession to Don White (who was the first in 1969), John Elders, John Burgess, Peter Colston, Mike Davis, Dick Greenwood and Martin Green. But for injury Uttley might have had an even more spectacular playing career. Between 1973 and 1980 he won 23 caps – and played in all four Grand Slam matches in 1980, except that he had to come off at half time against Wales. After retiring from playing in 1980 he emerged as a coach with the London Division and was appointed England coach in 1987. He is head of physical education at Harrow School.

32 Ian McGeechan of Scotland was the only one of the coaches from the four Home Unions to have first-hand knowledge of New Zealand and Australia prior to the 1991 World Cup. He was the senior coach on the British Lions' tour to Australia in 1989 (when the Test series was won 2–1) and went to New Zealand the following year with Scotland when the Scots pressed the All Blacks in both Tests. McGeechan had a distinguished playing career with Headingley, Scotland and the Lions, with whom he toured in 1974 and 1977. He is credited with creating the mental and physical framework which brought Scotland their Grand Slam in 1990.

33 Born in Caracas, Venezuela, in 1958, Serge Blanco was first recognized by the French rugby selectors 20 years later when he played for the "B" team against Wales at Aberavon. He has played on the wing and at full back, and has had the rare distinction of playing in two Grand Slam teams, 1981 and 1987. Blanco was in the French side which reached the first World Cup final in 1987, losing to New Zealand; the 1991 Grand Slam decider against England at Twickenham was his 85th appearance – a world record. He is still the potential match winner, a mercurial extra force behind the French backs. By sparking off the sort of length-of-the-pitch try which France scored against England in 1991 and by indulging in the kick and chase which brought him a try against Wales in the same championship, he has confounded those who think his career is over.

34 John Jeffrey, Scotland's White Shark, is captured in full flow on the attack against France in 1990. This was to be one of Jeffrey's most spectacular seasons, culminating in his supreme display in the Grand Slam decider against England at Murrayfield. A farmer in the Borders, Jeffrey has been playing for Scotland since 1984.

35 When John Rutherford retired in 1989, breaking his long-standing partnership with Roy Laidlaw, Scotland turned to Craig Chalmers of Melrose – and have continued with him ever since. Chalmers kicked three penalties in Scotland's Grand Slam-clinching 13–7 win over England in 1990. Now a stable choice and developing player, Chalmers is watched here by David Sole, Scotland's captain.

36 In 1991 Wales were in desperate need of players to help them rebuild; one of the men they turned to was Scott Gibbs, a 19-year-old centre with Neath, shown here in play against Ireland. The match ended in a 21–21 draw, giving Wales their only point in the championship – a slight improvement on the whitewash of 1990.

37 Simon Geoghegan, the London Irish wing, was one of the chief discoveries of the 1991 championship. His try against England early in the second half put Ireland ahead 7–3, forcing England to increase their efforts in a momentous finish. Born in England, he qualified for the Ireland team through his father. A law student, Geoghegan shows his try-scoring finish here against Wales.

38 David Campese is Australia's most-capped player and has appeared for them at full back and on the wing with equal effect. Born in 1962, he plays for the Randwick club in Sydney and for Milan. Campese is so unorthodox that even his own team mates do not know what he is going to do: "He can change pace and direction in a matter of inches," said Andy Slack, captain of the Australian team which won a Grand Slam on the tour of Britain and Ireland, "but you know if you have the ball he will be close by, looking to help." However, he remains capable of making critical errors – as in 1989 during the decisive third Test in Sydney when he allowed Ieuan Evans to make a vital touchdown which helped to swing the game.

39 Grant Fox is a phenomenal scoring machine for New Zealand. He broke into the All Blacks' team on a regular basis in the 1987 World Cup and apart from his directing matters at fly-half his goal-kicking has been a vital factor in the continued success of the side. He began the countdown to the World Cup in the summer of 1991 with the highest average of the top goal kickers. Born in 1962, Fox scored 119 points in the 1987 World Cup and in 1988 overtook Don Clarke's New Zealand record of 207 points which had stood for 24 years.

40 John Kirwan of New Zealand, 6ft. 2in. in height and weighing in at 14st. 7lb, is a genuine powerhouse wing. There is little subtlety about his playing style, it is simply his pace, his strength, his weight against the defence. Born in Auckland in 1964 he was first selected by New Zealand in 1984 at the age of 19. By the time he had played his 34th Test in 1989 he was New Zealand's record try-scorer – and could well be the leading try scorer in the 1991 World Cup.

CHAPTER 17

England turned to Steve Smith for their next captain. Smith was devastated by Beaumont's decision to quit, because he was a close personal friend, and while he knew that the decision was correct, he found it difficult to come to terms with the fact that Beaumont would not be back.

When Smith arrived at the Stourbridge training session at which Beaumont was an enforced spectator, Budge Rogers, the chairman of selectors, told him that he would be captain against Ireland. Smith had moved house that day, back into Cheshire, the county he captained in his first game for them when he was 18. At that time Smith was part of a Merseyside task force setting up training schemes for youngsters.

He had been preparing for an international along his usual lines – squash to sharpen up his footwork, sprints to help his speed off the mark and an eye on his diet so that he would go into the next game at 13st. "I live my life a stone underweight, you know," he said at the time. "I'm naturally a 14st. bloke and I can still put on seven pounds in a weekend. I'm like a jockey, really, trying to get it all off again."

Smith was an emotional character who cried when he first wore the England shirt. He cried in a different way, too, when Fran Cotton used to take him training, leading into their Grand Slam season. "Franny must like pain ... or he doesn't feel it," said Smith.

127

However, Ireland still had to be faced, and although there were all kinds of emotions involved in the England build-up, it did not produce an England win. Ireland, *en route* to their first Triple Crown since 1949, squeezed home 16–15 in a performance marked by a spectacular try from Gerry "Ginger" McLoughlin, a prop from Shannon. Props do not score spectacular tries very often at Twickenham and McLoughlin made the most of it.

Smith's leadership against Ireland had been a one-off appointment because the selectors had hoped Beaumont would be back. When it became clear that Beaumont would not return, England elected to stay with Smith for the match against France in Paris, which England won 27–15.

England were elated, especially with Hare's 19 points, and went to the after-match banquet in the Grand Hotel in high spirits. Each player had a gift of a bottle of aftershave at his dinner place. Maurice Colclough emptied away the aftershave and poured white wine in its place and made a great show of drinking the contents and challenging others to do so. The outcome was that Colin Smart, one of the Fngland front row, overdosed on aftershave and had to be taken to hospital to ensure that he suffered no severe damage. For that piece of behaviour the England players were warned about their future conduct.

Beating Wales 17–7 at Twickenham gave England joint second place in the championship table alongside Scotland. Hare, who was only a late substitute in Paris, kicked three penalties and England scored two tries through Carleton and Slemen. So Smith finished the season on a high note and also became England's most capped scrum-half . . . and set off to lead England on a high scoring tour of the United States and Canada. It was 43–6 over Canada, 59–0 over the USA, and the England mood was good.

At the start of the 1982–3 season another stage of the amateurism issue in rugby developed. It emerged that sports-wear manufacturers had been paying players to wear their goods – and that details of those payments were going to be presented to the Inland Revenue.

No names or payments ever came to the surface even though some of the names were said to be big and the payments even bigger. Whoever the players were who were involved – and the matter spread across the home countries – they remained silent. So did the Inland Revenue and the sportswear companies. No action was taken other than England players being asked to black out any markings on their boots so they could not be identified. Much later, when the Rugby Union did a deal with a manufacturer for all the England players to be identically equipped, all was said to be well.

The affair led to a division between the England players and the England selectors. Suspicion haunted that winter's activities, even though England continued the high-scoring from North America by wiping out Fiji 60–19 and then beating the Rest 47–7 in a trial. They were installed as favourites for the 1983 championship.

One of the more curious actions by the selectors early that season was to drop Mike Slemen, the left wing, after 29 caps. They did not give him a trial in which to state his case and confused the issue still further by replacing him with a right wing, Swift. After three games in the championship Swift was himself dropped ... for David Trick, also a right wing. It was a messy business and appeared to serve little purpose. England lost to France at Twickenham and then went to Cardiff to draw 13–13 with Wales, who had something of an experimental side in action under Eddie Butler's captaincy. Afterwards Budge Rogers heaped criticism for England's performance on the shoulders of the half backs, Smith and Cusworth. Both were dropped. Smith stood down for Nigel Melville but came back into the side when Melville was injured. Cusworth stayed out, replaced by Horton.

John Scott, the No. 8, was given the captaincy. Two shattering defeats followed, 12–22 against Scotland and 15–25

129

against Ireland, and England sank to the bottom of the table again with just that one point gained in Cardiff.

At the end of that season, Rogers retired as chairman of selectors and Davis as coach. They were succeeded by Derek Morgan, a dentist from Newbridge in South Wales who had played for England while still a student, and Dick Greenwood, the erudite Cambridge Blue, Lancastrian and schoolmaster.

The 1983 Lions tour to New Zealand followed. The word was that Peter Wheeler, the England hooker, who had hooked for three Tests in New Zealand in 1977 and four Tests in South Africa in 1980, was a certainty for captain. However, as John Pullin discovered in 1974, it is all very well being favourite for tour selection. The only people to be favourites with are selectors. Wheeler was not chosen, either as captain or player.

The Lions asked Ciaran Fitzgerald, the Irish hooker and captain, to lead the 18-match tour and they asked eight England players to travel as well. They also asked both England scrum-halves, Smith and Melville, to join the tour as replacements. Melville was injured and played two games. Smith, the 1980 Lions non-playing replacement, did manage to fit in two matches this time.

The Lions tour, with Willie John McBride as manager and Scotland's Jim Telfer as coach, was the shortest in history up to that time. Because of this there were fewer easy matches and less opportunity to work on problem areas because of the pressures of time.

The Lions were also up against an exceptional New Zealand team carefully led by Andy Dalton, a hooker and farmer, who had succeeded the outstanding Mourie. The All Blacks won the series 4-0, taking the final Test 38–6, and back at home Wheeler was about to discover that the year was not as sour as he might have first thought.

The new England management team moved quickly. Wheeler, after 36 caps, was made captain against Canada in October 1983, a crucial game in preparing England for the match against New Zealand at Twickenham the following month. Wheeler was also appointed captain of the Midlands.

The All Blacks came on tour, to Scotland and England, because a proposed trip to Argentina was called off. The New Zealanders did not bring the tight-five forwards from the squad which had beaten the Lions and neither did they bring David Loveridge, then the best scrum-half in the world. None of these players was available to travel, and New Zealand learned a painful lesson that you go nowhere these days unless the best players go.

England saw off Canada 27–0. Then Wheeler regrouped with the Midlands squad to prepare to play the All Blacks under the floodlights at Leciester, and they duly produced a fabulous win by 19–13, Dusty Hare kicking a penalty and dropping a goal to clinch the game. Subsequently seven of the Midlands side were chosen to play for England against New Zealand.

From Leicester the All Blacks went to Murrayfield to face Scotland. The Scots have never beaten New Zealand but took this match to a 25–25 draw with a late try from the Gosforth wing, Jim Pollock. It was unfortunate for Scotland that Peter Dods's conversion attempt from near to the posts went wide.

Now the revised England team faced the All Blacks. Slemen had been reinstated, on the left wing. Nick Youngs, a stocky farmer from East Anglia and the Leicester and Midlands scrum-half, partnered Cusworth at half back. England chose two new forwards, Colin White, a loose-head prop from Gosforth who was then 35 and knew the business of front-row play inside-out, and Paul Simpson, a flanker who was Yorkshire-born and had played a great deal in the North but was then a Bath player. Throughout the side England had experience and players with points to prove.

The All Blacks were a niggly team. They missed their anchor-men and they did not like being put under pressure. England were determined to make them suffer on both counts. There were many periods of rough play and England lost Carleton, the right wing, after a late tackle. Cuts proliferated and there was blood on many shirts. Wheeler led from the front but the most inspired England forward was Colclough. Youngs was in top form as well, and as England sensed that they could beat the All Blacks at home for the first time since 1936, the tension mounted.

It was 6–3 to England at half-time, two penalties against one, and in the second half Colclough barged through for a try from close range. Hare converted, and although New Zealand scored a try, a third penalty from Hare put England in final command at 15–9.

With only one change, Huw Davies for Paul Dodge at centre, England moved on to the 1984 championship, but all their hopes of a powerful start evaporated at Murrayfield against Scotland, who won the 100th game between the two countries 18–6. England scraped by 12–9 against Ireland in a match which introduced to the side a 20-year-old wing from Leicester, Rory Underwood, whose inclusion meant, finally, that Slemen was out.

Underwood scored his first try for England in the next game, against France, capitalizing on a dribble to run on and score, but otherwise England laboured for lengthy periods in Paris and were beaten 32–18. With Wales winning 24–15 at Twickenham the England season ended on another low note. Meanwhile the Scots, under Jim Aitken's captaincy, forged their first Grand Slam for 59 years with a win over France before a passionately excited crowd in the final game at Murrayfield.

A few days after the championship ended, England announced that they would undertake a tour to South Africa that summer. The decision was taken against a wide body of external opposition but the Rugby Union vote was heavily in favour of the tour. The tour manager was not, as expected, Derek Morgan, the chairman of selectors who was appointed assistant manager. The trip was headed by Ron Jacobs, the president of the Rugby Union. The tour captain was John

Scott. The list of unavailable players mounted until it reached 18 and it became clear that the tour might be a playing disaster.

CHAPTER 18

One of the important shifts of emphasis in English rugby in 1984 was in the Cup competition – known at that time as the John Player Special Cup. From its first year in 1972, six clubs had won the Cup outright – Gloucester, Coventry, Bedford, Gosforth, Leicester and Bristol – while in 1982 Moseley shared the trophy with Gloucester.

Leicester, under the astute coaching of Charlie White, had won in three successive finals from 1979 and their style, attitude and quality of support all contributed to the growing stature of the competition. White was such a successful coach that he would have merited the national job, but it never came his way, and he went on to become technical administrator for the South West.

Jack Rowell was another coach to admire. He had been at the helm with Gosforth, his home club, before they won the Cup in 1977 and 1978. Then he joined Bath, who were still operating in the shadow of their West Country rivals, Bristol and Gloucester. Soon after Rowell's arrival, Bath won 26 matches in succession to round off a season in which they scored more than 1,000 points.

The year 1984 marked the real breakthrough for Bath. Not only did they reach the Cup final at Twickenham for the first time, they also beat the holders Bristol 10–9 in a compelling contest.

Bath were led by Roger Spurrell, a curly-haired and amiable flanker whose method of captaincy was to be out ahead of his men, showing the way. Spurrell thought all along that Bath had the team to win, and with a 10–3 lead at half-time, his confidence was justified. Bristol closed the gap to a single point with a try by Richard Harding, their scrum-half, with 25 minutes still to play, but there was no more scoring on an afternoon when the wind cut teasingly across the ground, testing the skills of goal-kickers on both sides.

Jack Rowell rarely stays in one place when he is watching a game and with a few minutes to go was observed to leave his seat because the tension had become unbearable. He was believed to be in the car park when Bristol had their final chance to save the game – a penalty. The kicker was the Bristol fly-half Stuart Barnes, then 21. He had already played for Welsh Schools and Newport and had been in a Welsh Rugby Union squad before opting for England, the country of his birth. Despite all that, Barnes missed the goal, leaving Bath the winners.

Bath's success was mirrored in the England tour party to South Africa. They provided David Trick, John Palmer, John Horton, Richard Hill and Jon Hall. Barnes, a clear candidate, was not available. Overall, the tour party was astonishingly thin on players with Test experience.

The Rugby Union's decision to go to South Africa was taken on the eve of the county championship final at Twickenham when Gloucestershire beat Somerset 36–18. This final marked the return of the county championship to Twickenham on a regular basis and eight players who took part were selected for the tour.

At the same time, world rugby was carrying on as normal despite a prediction a few months earlier that the game was about to turn professional on a global basis, with 200 players poised to sign for an organization which would have been titled "World Championship Rugby". The plan had been brought to London by an Australian radio commentator and would-be impresario named David Lord, who said that the scheme was well advanced and that the 1984 international championship would be the last of its kind.

Lord and his scheme came under close examination in the cellars of the Cheshire Cheese public house in London's Fleet Street, when the rugby writers of the day grilled the affable Australian on all aspects of the venture. It never took off, but those who laughed at the proposals should have done so in the knowledge that some groundwork had been undertaken and that, if professional rugby union did not emerge at that juncture, there were still people around who considered that it might in the future.

So England set off for South Africa, flying non-stop from London to Johannesburg, to play seven matches of which only three offered anything like known and full-strength opposition – the two Tests and the game with Western Province at Cape Town. The South African Rugby Board was so grateful that England had agreed to travel that they would have fallen in line with any demands for fixtures. England wanted to play against black and coloured players and to see that South African rugby was developing along multi-racial lines, and that is what they were allowed to do.

This was one of the reasons why Errol Tobias seemed to be playing against England in every match. Then aged 34, this fly-half from Boland had been on the international scene for 12 years and was widely recognized as one of the best black players to emerge in South Africa. In all, he played four times against England during the tour.

England won their two warm-up games and then put in a sterling performance against Western Province, who fielded a pack which appeared to contain five earth-movers and three tractors. England hung in against this huge amount of flesh and scored two tries against one. They were denied victory on somewhat tenuous grounds when Trick was judged to have obstructed his opposite number and the penalty gave Western Province a 15–15 draw.

There was much optimism in the England camp that evening but the full South African side represented an entirely different challenge for the England side. Scott and the tour selectors produced a team containing five new caps – Palmer, Hill and Mark Bailey in the backs, Malcolm Preedy and Chris Butcher in the forwards.

Butcher came from a rugby-playing family and was something of a rugby itinerant, playing year round in both hemispheres, but he had picked up some valuable experience of life as well as of rugby on his various trips and came into his first cap at No. 8, standing 6ft 5in and weighing 15$\frac{1}{2}$st. He was quick, confident and chatty, and Scott, England's most capped No. 8 who was ahead of him in the second row, was given to understand that Butcher was the coming man.

The first Test was at Port Elizabeth and the Springboks, themselves rusty from inactivity and decreased contact with world rugby, took time to establish control. They were ahead 18–12 with 20 minutes left but finally rammed home their superiority 33–15.

The second Test at Ellis Park, Johannesburg, was one week later. Everyone knew that on a short tour England had to pin their hopes on winning the first Test and establish some kind of psychological and physical superiority. The Springboks' victory by such a clear margin made it obvious that something of a repeat was heading England's way. England responded by changing the entire front row but retained the rest of the players with the exception of the wing, where Tony Swift came in for Trick.

England were suffering before they began. In the early stages Butcher had a colourful fight with one of the Springbok forwards. John Fidler, all heart in the second row alongside Scott, had a knee injury and was not fully fit but played on with total resolution. So did others, notably Peter Winterbottom at flanker, a new hooker from Coventry named Steve Brain, and a new flanker from Nottingham, Gary Rees, who came on for the last 20 minutes.

However, the main story of the day was the Springbok forwards grinding out their supremacy and their backs running through an increasingly tiring and exasperated defence. In a record 35–9 victory, South Africa scored six tries, three of them by Danie Gerber, a phenomenal centre of great strength and pace.

In the short-term the tour offered England little. The individual successes were few and just seven of the tour party played in the next international against Australia the following November when Butcher, much heralded that year, in fact played his final game for England.

In the long-term Hill, after some turbulent times, was the No. 1 scrum-half six years later. Paul Rendall, Rees, Hall and Winterbottom forged on as England contenders, as, in the end, did Mike Teague, who played three games on the tour but was definitely a second choice for the back-row positions.

Scott did not appear for England again. His captaincy record was: played four, lost four – undeserved for a man who contributed so much to England rugby. He played on with Cardiff, providing great service. Fidler was not required again and neither was Hare, the kicker supreme, who scored 240 points in his 25 international appearances. Hare went back to Leicester and kicked on and on into retirement, finally, in 1989.

CHAPTER 19

By the time Will Carling transferred from Terra Nova, in 1979, he was already nationally known and the schools' grapevine already assured that Sedbergh knew what they were receiving. There were those at Terra Nova who wondered what would happen to his rugby, none more so than Michael Hope and Ian Argyle, both on the staff at Terra Nova, who were among the first to appreciate Carling's abilities.

"I was deputy head and in charge of rugby and I ran the first XV," says Argyle, now head of the Aldro School in the peaceful village of Shackleford, Surrey. "I used to run a young training squad, once a week, and it was there that I first saw Will play. I said at the time that there could not be a seven-year-old who could do what he could with a rugby ball. He had exceptional handling and his kicking was already impressive. He just stood out."

Carling was known as "Carling ii" at Terra Nova; brother Marcus, ahead of him, was "Carling i". The name of Carling ii figured in all kinds of sporting achievements and in five terms in the first XV he played 42 matches and scored 24 tries. In that same period he was in ten seven-a-side tournaments, scoring 13 tries.

In 1979 Terra Nova travelled to the prestigious Rosslyn Park national schools sevens in south-west London with a team which they thought would win the preparatory schools event. They were stopped in the quarter finals in muddy going by Llanarth Court, but the excitement of the day never left Carling's memory. He still loves sevens. Argyle loved watching Carling play sevens as well, and when in 1989 he set up a sevens tournament at Aldro School he donated the Carling Cup for the winners – in appreciation of all the enjoyment which Will Carling had provided.

There were other school feats which Carling achieved – the record for the 400 metres in 66 seconds, the record for the long jump at 4.3 metres and throwing the cricket ball for 40.25 metres. In 1978, when he won the cricket trophy, he took 36 wickets for 348 runs in 160.2 overs, almost three times as many overs as any other player. Yes, Sedbergh were taking on a sportsman all right.

Sedbergh was founded in 1525, almost 300 years before rugby football was formally created at Rugby School. If Sedbergh is approached from the east it is difficult not to be refreshed by the rugged grandeur of the surrounding countryside as the road winds and dips and rises through the unchanging splendour of the Yorkshire Dales National Park. A former head of the school, questioned about playground facilities, is said to have replied: "We have the finest in England, forty square miles." Sedbergh has been a rugby-playing school since 1879, when masters and boys combined to play against local sides.

The first recorded game was against Kendal. It ended in a draw when darkness stopped play, and in 1880 there was a game which involved Sedbergh boys playing for both teams – the participants being Cumberland and Westmorland versus the World.

Ampleforth have been opponents of Sedbergh since the start, and one hundred years on, John Willcox, a former England full back in charge of rugby at Ampleforth, wrote these words of Sedbergh: "Year in, year out, your XVs epitomise everything that is good in rugby football, deep commitment, a refreshing desire to run and run, a determination which never admits of being beaten, and enviable stamina, speed and skill, and most importantly of all a friend-liness and ease of manner after a game which makes you as generous in victory as in defeat: the laughter afterwards is always there.

"Brown" may be a terrifying cry to others but it is a cry of which you should be very proud. Brown, brown shirts, brown stockings, a sound and sight which down the years has struck awe if not fear into many redoubtable opponents. The flash of brown as another crushingly low tackle hurls an opponent to the ground is vivid in my memory. Of all the impressions that I have, this above all stands out; and I would judge Sedbergh as a school which produces the finest tackling sides I have ever seen. This comparison is made bearing in mind many of the best schoolboy sides in the four home countries.

"For those of us who think that schoolboy rugby is the best by far to watch, with its complete disregard for percentage or safety first tactics, with its accent on attack and attack and if that fails attack again, with its very unexpected twists and turns, with its intense rivalry and burgeoning skill, Sedbergh is an outstanding advertisement."

Sedbergh had been producing boys who went on to play rugby for England since 1906 – three of whom became captain: Lord Wakefield, John Spencer and Carling. To date eleven England players were at Sedbergh, 16 Scottish internationals and two Irish. All of them would have played on Busk Holme, the main pitch, where the Wavell Wakefield pavilion now stands. Inside, on the honours board, are the records of Sedbergh's rugby history with the players' initials in red, their surnames in black. In the home dressing room sit 17 rugby balls on a rack, like giant eggs, and it is from this room that all the first XVs run out, wearing the famous brown shirt to which John Willcox referred.

Carling spent his first year in a dormitory then moved on to his own room. He was allocated to Winder House, named after a dominant hill at Sedbergh. It was the furthest house from the centre of the school, as Carling was made aware when the weather turned bleak and bitter. Once the rugby pitch received six feet of rainfall in a season.

His house tutor at Winder was John Morris. "Will was one of a group of about a dozen new boys who came to Winder," he recalls. "They used to come in a day ahead of the other boys and on the very first afternoon would be playing touch rugby. Will came with his grandmother and it was clear he was not going to be overawed – he had quite a lot of confidence. There would be a big turn-out of staff to watch the new-boy rugby trials and Will came in with some good players – Julian Cheetham, a wing, Andrew Sayner, Guy Yeoman and Tim Thorpe – who established themselves immediately and all progressed to the first XV.

"Will's handling skills were there and so was his ability to time a pass. It is all so obvious in touch rugby and although small boys can be incredibly selfish with the ball I never remember Will being like that. Of course he was immediately spotted and promoted within the framework.

"As his tutor for five years I was responsible for seeing him about his work, behaviour and attitude, based on a regular reporting system. He was one in his year group who people looked up to because he was a star games player and he was in a very influential position for good or bad. Rugby is a macho thing and the good player can do a lot of good by being approachable and friendly, but he can also be quite destructive because his self-importance and position of strength in the peer groups can make him behave in an unpleasant way. Guy Yeoman was always Will's rival when it came down to positions of responsibility. They had a rivalry throughout their school career and Yeoman went on to become head of school. By the time Will left school he understood about human relations but people were a bit frightened of him because he was so successful."

Carling had been used to playing with older boys at Terra Nova and the same thing happened at Sedbergh. His last three years were in the first XV and they lost just one match in one season and were unbeaten in the other two. Referring to the 1983–4 season, the *Sedberghian* noted: "Behind them and usually making the half break for them was W.D.C. Carling whose success with last year's England Schools already had him marked out as something exceptional. At full back this year he found room to express himself in delightful and unselfish style which brought the very best out of his colleagues and turned a good side into another all-conquering one."

Kerry Wedd, who coached the Sedbergh first XV at the time, says of Carling: "My memory of him as a player at school is that he always wanted to turn a defensive situation into an attacking one. He wanted to turn every opportunity there was into a try-scoring situation. If we every disagreed it was over that – I wanted to be safe and he did not. He instilled this attitude into all the youngsters around him and it was something he had from his early days. Other influences have shaped his game since he left Sedbergh but put him into a close situation and he will become world-class because of his reflexes and judgement of space. His special gift is that when he is closed down in a no-hope situation he is still able to do something."

As Carling progressed through Sedbergh, the reports on him changed in emphasis from being critical of the need to "strike a more even balance between his games and his work" and that "he will have to be careful how he uses his influence, being prepared to tolerate some of the less gifted members of the community", to eventual praise in his final two years. A year before he left he was described as follows: "Potentially he has the power of leadership."

Others began to take note of Carling's skills. He was invited to play for Yorkshire Schools – although Sedbergh is now in Cumbria its allegiance in school sport remains with Yorkshire – and led them on a tour to Zimbabwe in 1984.

Academically, his results were respectable, and when he completed his five years at Sedbergh he had "A" level passes in geography, economics and English. Overall, what emerged during Carling's time at Sedbergh was that he was a young man on the rise.

He had been outstanding at rugby at school and he had been almost as successful at cricket. If there was one thing at Sedbergh to which Carling did not commit as much as other activities it was fell running. Sedbergh has something called the "Wilson Run", named after its founder Bernard Wilson who began it in 1881. Baugh Fell, described in that first year as uneven, tussocky and often boggy ground, characteristic of the moorland, and Muddy Slide, the severest climb, are just two parts of a course which is thought to have originated from a paper chase.

When Carling ran in that event, John Morris was slightly irritated that he did not train properly for it. Carling finished 125th in more than one hour and 45 minutes. Perhaps they should have put a rugby ball in his hands.

CHAPTER 20

Schoolboy teams and their selection at national level owe much to the consistency and clear thinking of the men responsible. Those selected for England Schools have often gone on to greater things in significant numbers and in 1983, when Carling was introduced to this England stage, three went on to win full caps and a fourth made the England squad.

Since 1975 there has been a Grand Slam available to the schoolboys of England, Wales, Ireland, Scotland and France. By 1983 England had won the junior Slam twice, and in Carling's first season there was the opportunity to do so again.

England beat Ireland 16–0 at Moseley, France 34–0, and Scotland 20–3 at Aberdeen, which took them to a showdown with Wales, who were also unbeaten, at Pontypridd. Carling had scored two tries on the way, while England had conceded none, and he went to Wales for the first time in his life thinking that he would be in a side which achieved a clean sweep.

Ian Gibson, who was coach to the England team, recalls: "It was close all the way through and we lost our No. 8 about 20 minutes from the end with a broken leg. We had territorial advantage and the better backs but Wales had a stronger back row. We could have won the match when Carling went for the corner from about 20 yards out, but he was judged to have put his foot in touch a yard from the Welsh line. We lost on a penalty from 40 yards."

Carling has always disputed the verdict that he put a foot into touch. The one thing he did learn from the 12–13 defeat was how much Welsh teams liked beating England.

He hung on to his first England Schools shirt as a memento but more were to follow. In 1983 he played alongside Kevin Simms of Liverpool, who led the team in three matches and by one of those curious twists was Carling's co-centre when he made his senior debut in Paris in 1988.

The following year Carling was made captain. "The boys would always respect a captain who played the year before," explains Gibson, "and Will must have learned and seen a lot in 1983. You are reliant on a lot of information from other people when you choose a captain, and you base your choice on fairly limited knowledge. You almost have to listen outside the dressing room door to hear what the candidates are saying. Will was one of those rare choices which is made because of previous experience, because he will lead, and because the others want to be led by him.

"The first match in which he was captain was against Wales at Cambridge. Will came to myself and Dick Tilley, who was helping with the coaching, and said that the players should be allowed to go to the cinema on the eve of the match. We said they could – but asked if they had any tickets for the coaches which, of course, they hadn't. We know that they did not go anywhere near to a cinema. They went to a pub, saw the landlord and arranged a special room for themselves. It was extraordinary that a 17-year-old captain should do that. He was concerned that they might not be together off the field."

England beat Wales 18–0. That gave Carling instant satisfaction and the chance to continue a rivalry with the Welsh scrum-half, Robert Jones of Cwmtawe, who led Wales that year. He and Carling would be in opposition at the highest level only a few seasons later.

Next England were taken apart by Ireland in Belfast, losing

7–15. The England forwards suffered badly and Kerry Wedd of Sedbergh observed of Carling that day: "He was desperate for success for the whole lot of them. Will was in a formative time and didn't take it particularly well. He has always had the ability to give it all and his concentration while it is on is phenomenal. People take it as over-competitive but is is not that. It is just winning or losing, the satisfaction of doing the job properly."

There was one game left for England Schools that year, against France in St Nazaire. Gibson saw it this way: "We were behind to France on a very hot day, so hot you needed salt tablets and lots of water. We were still behind at full time, there was a band playing and we missed a penalty. It was so noisy that the referee ordered the kick to be re-taken and this time it went over and we were 10–12 behind.

"In those conditions, with heat and a hooting, whistling crowd Will kept the side going well. Very late [in injury time] we ran a ball from just outside the 22. It was a back-row move down the narrow side with Wilby and Blackmore, on to Buzza who was the fly-half, then Priestley and finally Carling took the ball, with space. He went for the gap hard and timed his pass well to Bennett whose try won the match. I was running down the touchline with my son Russell, shouting myself hoarse."

Gibson was born near Wakefield. He studied at Loughborough Colleges and played club rugby at centre for Northampton, Leicester and Wakefield and for Yorkshire in the county championship. He had two England trials. In 1983, when Carling was first in the Schools side, Gibson was in his 19th and final year at Doncaster Grammar School and is now a senior housemaster at Blew House in Dulwich College, south-east London. He is director of physical education and in charge of rugby.

Gibson had an eleven-year involvement with England schoolboy sides at 16 and 18 age-group levels. He saw Carling first in the Yorkshire side and was impressed that a slim

147

player tackled more than his weight, the outstanding feature of Carling's game at the time.

"Carling and I had a very professional relationship rather than a friendly one," says Gibson. "It is a critical time for these boys because they have to play games in quick succession over the Easter holiday and they all have exams coming up. There has been a demise in the state schools as far as producing talent is concerned but we still see a hell of a lot of kids playing in the independent and public schools. We have this terrific advantage of thousands of players.

"In the mid-fifties and sixties the grammar schools were at their peak for providing players and with Mike Davis as coach we beat Wales 26–0 at Cardiff with a lot of state schoolboys. Ten years on the side mostly contained boys from public schools.

"When you coach the 16 group you realize that whatever you say, they regard as gospel and you have to be careful you are on the right lines. At 18 they have minds of their own and what you want from them is self-discipline, especially off the field. They should always be immaculate and think for themselves – I regarded that as one of my pet themes.

"The player who does not make a decision does not deserve to be an international, and one of the things we said to Will Carling was that, whatever you do we will go along with it. You may make mistakes but come back and let's talk about it. In that way you improve.

"It was always my ambition to coach England Schools. Will must have been immensely proud to be captain at that stage of his career. If you are made captain at anything the first reaction is one of immense surprise, then being proud, and then being worried about how you will cope. But to get into the national side at whatever level you must have a certain amount of arrogance and realize you are pretty extraordinary.

"I did not see Will Carling for four years. Then just after he was made captain of England, in 1988, he came to Dulwich College to watch a match. He arrived wearing a cricket sweater, and we walked around, chatted and stood behind the posts. I asked if he would have a word with the lads afterwards. "What shall I say to them?" he asked. That's humility for you. He went in and criticized them for not running straight. He picked up on an area where he was confident."

After the summer of 1984, Will Carling was given a round-the-world air ticket by his parents, £100 in spending money, and departed for Hong Kong, Singapore, Australia, New Zealand, Hawaii and the West coast of the USA. He washed up and welded and drove a sand buggy in high temperatures in the parched desert of Australia and moved on to New Zealand where he washed up, yet again, on a farm and finally made his way home. He came back wearing a T-shirt which carried the words "Hooray Henry the Pom".

Kerry Wedd says: "The year off was vital to him. He needed to find himself. He went as a youngster and came back as a young man, just two different people. He was prepared to do that, to get away from constant demands and all that adrenaline which pumped through when he was playing rugby. He needed a break because it was a pressure time for a young fellow. He always knew he was coming back ... to go for it."

In the autumn of 1985, back from his world trip, Carling went to Durham University on an army scholarship with the Royal Regiment of Wales. He had appeared before a Regular Commissions Board for a variety of interviews and tests before he was offered a place. He went to Durham as a second-lieutenant to read psychology with the intention of serving for five years when he graduated.

He had put on weight during his travels and was slightly concerned that total absence from rugby might have affected him. His time at Durham University was to show that his fears were groundless, while his chosen subject, psychology, was to eventually to help him in his task of leading England.

CHAPTER 21

While Carling departed for points East, including Australia, the Australian rugby team was on its way to Britain for an 18-match tour which was to be both unique and sad. It was unique because this Australian side, captained by Andrew Slack, a three-quarter from Queensland, beat all four home countries. It was sad because incoming tours after this one were never again to incorporate all four home countries and consequently the Grand Slam was no longer an option.

Unlike New Zealand teams, who want to win every game, the Australians knew that they had a first team and then not much else, and as a result did not seriously object when their midweek team ran into trouble. They lost four midweek matches and were unconvincing in others, but in the Tests they had very few problems and the closest result was their 16–9 win over Ireland.

While the Australians might be remembered for the quality and sense of adventure of their runners and the great skill of their fly-half Mark Ella, the one person who made a real impact was their coach, Alan Jones. On every issue, major or minor, Jones had a view. If there was no issue he was capable of creating one. He had one of the fastest minds and fastest tongues most people in rugby had experienced and took his task extremely seriously. He met every challenge head-on, while his meticulous preparation was vital to the successes of the tour.

Not only did Jones oversee the Grand Slam tour, he took Australia on to a key victory over New Zealand in 1986 and to the World Cup in 1987 where his players looked certain of a place in the final until they were overhauled by France in a mammoth semi-final comeback in Sydney.

Jones did not know much about rugby from direct playing experience, but he could hone in on aspects of the game which required development, and if there were any weaknesses in his knowledge they were difficult to detect. He also had intense commitment to his players, and made a point of having a full knowledge and understanding of all who played for him.

Jones had been a political speech-writer and could out-talk anyone on almost any issue. It was not surprising that the high profile he obtained through coaching Australia was one of the reasons why he became the anchor-man of one of the nation's leading radio shows.

Nobody in Britain knew what to expect from Jones when he arrived for that tour but he charged into business on a high-octane level, demanding this, seeking that, with almost everything being done on the run. He was refreshingly differ-ent, from the great variety of methods in his training sessions to the way he actually seemed to see into players' minds, probing for ways to help them improve and contribute more to the team.

A few days before the Australians arrived, England lost to a President's XV in a match which commemorated 75 years of rugby at Twickenham. Against Australia, though, in the opening international of the tour, England made six changes and introduced five new caps.

Nigel Melville finally made it to the pitch in an England jersey. He was also given the captaincy on his debut, at 23 the youngest player to achieve that double. He went in with a new fly-half in Barnes. The other new cap outside the scrum was Rob Lozowski of Wasps at centre, who was not

151

chosen again, while in the forwards Bath's position in the game was reflected by the selection of Gareth Chilcott at prop and Nigel Redman, aged 20, at lock. Bath and Wasps each provided three players – Barnes had not then moved over from Bristol. For the first time, the England bench included a fly-half from Cambridge University, Rob Andrew, who had already played for the England under-23 team.

Barnes kicked a penalty in the first half, matching one by Michael Lynagh for Australia, but England did not score again. Early in the second half Ella, well screened by his centres running ahead of him, broke through for a try and the floodgates opened: Australia went on to win 19–3. Considering that Lynagh missed a number of goal kicks England escaped lightly, but the home side was never properly in the hunt for possession, especially in the line-out, and coach Dick Greenwood lamented: "We are an immature side which has not grown or developed together. I hope it gets the chance to do so."

In the second Test, against Ireland, Australia recovered from 6–9 behind to win 16–9 and again it was a try by Ella which altered the course of the match. Australia only became certain of victory in the final moments – a situation which the Australians did not permit to happen again.

Against a poor Welsh team, the Wallabies came through 28–9 and included in their four tries was a pushover which has gone into the annals of Australian rugby as one of the most significant scores ever made. Then, against Scotland, who had won the Grand Slam only a few months earlier, Australia scored four tries for a record 37–12 win.

Although Ella was the inspiration behind the Australian back play, proper credit had to be given to the Wallaby pack which included men chosen specifically for the scrummaging tests which they expected in Britain and Ireland. The Australians were fortunate to have the skills of Enrique "Topo" Rodriguez, an Argentine international, the 16st. Tommy Lawton and Andy McIntyre in their front row, and the 6ft 7in. Steve Cutler in their second row.

152

The Australians had barely left for home when Romania arrived for a three-match tour, culminating in a first international at Twickenham. The North were the first opposition, at Birkenhead Park, and Andrew set them on the road to a 17–8 win with a try after 15 minutes.

Another significant moment in that match came after 22 minutes of the second half. Jim Syddall, the Waterloo lock, was injured and had to be replaced; the man who came on was Wade Dooley of the Preston Grasshoppers club. None of the spectators could fail to notice Dooley waiting eagerly to go on to the pitch, because he stood 6ft 8ins and weighed close to 18st.

Dooley was then aged 27 and had been playing for Preston Grasshoppers for eight years. At school he had played Rugby League and appeared for Warrington Schoolboys. He had been in Rugby Union for a long time without being properly recognized but in 1984 he became a regular choice with Lancashire. The few minutes he played for the North against Romania were enough to project Dooley towards a first cap against Romania on 5 January 1985.

Andrew was called up for his first cap as well, and so was his scrum-half, Richard Harding of Bristol. The captaincy switched to Paul Dodge at centre, and only four players who were original choices against Australia began against Romania.

For Andrew the match started on a high note because England came hurtling out of defence from the kick-off with Andrew, Dodge and Underwood to the fore. England won a line-out and Andrew dropped a goal – all in 44 seconds! The match continued more predictably after that, England winning 22–15, scoring their one try two minutes from the end. Andrew kicked four penalties and dropped two goals and was entitled to think that he had arrived.

Dooley was also entitled to think so, but he was wise enough to realize that he was off the pace against Romania and set to work to improve his fitness. He was helped by the fact that the championship matches were partially rearranged that winter after a spell of bad weather and England did not play again until the following month. Dooley has missed only a handful of matches since then and has become England's most capped second row forward.

The 1985 championship brought more bad news for England. They did force a draw, 9–9, with France at Twickenham but had a tremendous escape when Patrick Esteve, the flier from Narbonne on the French wing, was worked over the England line and took so long to decide to touch down that Harding was able to scamper back and ensure that Esteve lost the ball in the tackle.

France were nearly penalized out of existence in the second half but did not suffer unduly for it in terms of goal-kicking chances against them. In fact the day was probably most significant for Chris Martin, the Bath full back, who made his first appearance for England, and for Teague, who came off the bench to win his first cap midway through the second half.

The changes because of the weather kept England at Twickenham for their next game, against Scotland, and this produced their only win; the Scots finished the season with a whitewash, one year after their Grand Slam. England beat them 10–7 but had another escape when Scotland, chasing a kick-through by Peter Dods, had the horrific experience of three unmarked players hunting the ball and all of them over-running it.

None of that was particularly good for England's nerves, and the match against Ireland in Dublin proved to be another which hung on a last-minute incident – except in this case Ireland won. England had a 10–7 lead after 19 minutes of the second half but this was cancelled out by a penalty by Mike Kiernan with just five minutes to go. With seconds left Kiernan dropped a goal to win the game, and the Triple Crown.

The final game took England to Cardiff. Wales gave first caps to Jonathan Davies at fly-half and Phil Davies at No. 8. Davies was then a Neath player and Phil Davies was a Llanelli player but everyone in Wales thought that they would be fixtures in the team for a long time to come. The match also marked the first appearance for Wales at Cardiff of Paul Thorburn, a young full back from Neath.

For a while the day offered England the chance at last to win at Cardiff. They were ahead after just one minute when Andrew kicked a penalty and led twice more in the first half, after putting Simon Smith on a 20-yard run for a try, and after Andrew kicked a second penalty.

England had the lead for a fourth time after 15 minutes of the second half with a dropped goal from Andrew. Then Jonathan Davies decided to step on to the stage. He sent up a towering kick to the England posts and Martin, lonely and unsupported, could not deal with the ball. Davies came in to score a try and put Wales ahead for the first time. The final score was 24–15 to Wales and their captain Terry Holmes said: "People were talking as though it was our divine right to win at home. But we came back and ended the season on a high note."

Shortly before the championship ended the International Rugby Football Board met in Paris and agreed to a proposal to stage the first World Cup in Australia and New Zealand in 1987. From that point on, rugby football was to make a fundamental change in its character, the biggest alteration in its existence. By progressing to a four-year cycle of competition, like the Olympic Games and the soccer World Cup, rugby was to increase both the players' aspirations and the demands on them as never before.

CHAPTER 22

Having played South Africa twice in 1984 and Australia once, England next faced a tour to New Zealand in the summer of 1985. Dick Greenwood was not available to coach the side, and England turned to another ex-Cambridge University man, Martin Green, son of an England trialist named "Pinky" Green who carried on playing until he was nearly 60. Most of Green's club rugby was with Moseley at flanker, while in coaching he had come up via the Midlands side to the England under-23 and "B" teams.

Green was not an England player but always said that would not inhibit his coaching. He went into the job believing that he had a close identity with the players, and not only did he know the game well but that he knew the players better. Coaching, he contended, was having the skill to spot what was going right or wrong and the knowledge to realize what to do next. He was also fully aware that on a tour to New Zealand England needed some early successes in the provincial games to secure a victory in a Test.

England operated a two-coach system for the first time because Brian Ashton, who had been coaching the colts, was brought in to work with the backs. Derek Morgan was appointed manager and Dodge continued as captain. The final selection was affected by the unavailability of some regular choices, including Andrew and Underwood. Against that, England were able to include Steve Bainbridge, the Gosforth lock, who had ruled himself out of selection for the domestic season because he had been sent off. Bainbridge had been to New Zealand on the 1983 Lions tour and knew the country and its rugby well. So did Jamie Salmon, who won three caps for New Zealand in 1981. However, in the rest of the squad of 26 there was a desperate shortage of knowledge of New Zealand – not surprisingly, because it was 12 years since an England side had visited the country.

England began with two wins, against North Auckland and Poverty Bay, but came to understand a little more about the qualities of the New Zealand game when they were defeated 24–6 by Auckland, the provincial champions. Auckland's selectors knew what they were doing because it became apparent much later that six of the side which played England then were almost certain starters for the New Zealand World Cup team six years ahead.

The touring side came in for a fair amount of praise from Andy Haden, the Auckland captain and spokesman on just about everything sporting in New Zealand, who described the England line-out work via Dooley and Bainbridge as the best he had seen on the Eden Park ground for a long time. John Hart, the Auckland coach, did not dismiss England either for the first Test. "They will give the All Blacks the hurry-up if they use possession a little more wisely," he said.

England responded to Haden's comments on their line-out play by leaving out Dooley and playing John Orwin, the RAF fitter from Gloucester. Although they had brought two full backs on the tour, they switched Huw Davies, nominally a fly-half, and capped three players for the first time – Salmon, Mike Harrison, the Wakefield and Yorkshire wing, and Paul Huntsman, a prop from Headingley.

England played a terrific first Test at Christchurch for more than an hour. Harrison made an immediate impact because, as New Zealand attacked in the 23rd minute, hurling men in numbers towards the England line, he intercepted a loopy pass and sprinted some 50 metres for a try. A second

England try was scored by Teague who was first to a chip to the corner by Melville, and England led 13–12 at half-time.

Much defiance came from the England ranks and they continued to hold out all New Zealand attacks, but they could not curb the threat from the goal-kicking of Kieran Crowley, the All Blacks full back, whose boot became decisive.

When Dodge was adjudged offside after 22 minutes of the second half, Crowley kicked his fifth penalty to claim the lead for New Zealand and he kicked another penalty near to the end to make the result 18–13. Crowley had not played for New Zealand at this level before. A farmer from Taranaki, he has a set of goalposts on his land so that he can practice goal kicking. England found how proficient he had become.

The crowd at Christchurch had totalled around 25,000, poor by New Zealand standards, and not all of them wanted to watch the match. New Zealand were due to tour South Africa that year; the trip was later called off but protesters managed to throw tennis balls filled with tacks on to the pitch. Someone else put a hoax bomb in a cistern in the ground. Elsewhere an attempt was made to disrupt post office communications at a relay station; and the discreet police guard on England remained.

The teams re-grouped for the second Test the following Saturday, this time at Wellington. Both sides repeated their selections. The referee, Kerry Fitzgerald of Australia, was also the same, but everything else was different.

New Zealand did not expect England to raise their game above the level of the first Test, but Andy Dalton, captain of the All Blacks, reckoned that his team had much more to give, granted the benefit of one match together, the assessment of that performance and the work which followed in training. They did not intend to be caught again.

England put a try in after only two minutes, driving in on a bad clearance from a line-out for Jon Hall to score. But the All Blacks started scoring shortly after, and by half-time were pulling away at 13–9. There was sporadic fighting and

158

Steve Brain, the England hooker, carried a head wound for most of the match. However, the greatest blows to England came with the frequent New Zealand scores in the second half.

The All Blacks twice drove scrums to win touchdowns. England fell further and further behind, briefly halting the pattern when Harrison scored from an interception, mirroring his first Test effort; but it was a forlorn team which came off at the end, beaten 42–15, the heaviest defeat in England's history.

Melville had lasted until half-time and came off with hamstring injuries. He was replaced by Hill. Orwin limped off midway through the second half, which allowed Dooley on. Nine of the 17 England players were found to need treatment afterwards. Three of the All Blacks were hurt. The English players eventually shrugged off the effects of the rough play and their belief that the referee did nothing to stop it. What they could not shrug off were the statistics. In five successive Tests against Southern Hemisphere opposition in a year, England had lost every time, conceding 147 points and 18 tries against 55 points and four tries.

As it turned out, the match in Wellington was the last between England and New Zealand for six years. They missed playing each other in the 1987 World Cup because England could not beat Wales in the quarter finals and no other matches were arranged before the 1991 World Cup, when they were drawn to meet in the opening game.

Before the 1985–86 season began, England appointed Mike Weston as chairman of selectors and World Cup team manager, giving him slightly under two years to prepare the groundwork and head the operation. He was the first manager to be so titled and stressed from the outset: "This is not the Mike Weston show. This game is all about players and coaches and selectors. I see my job in the background."

Weston also saw as a priority a squad of 45 players being assembled within a matter of weeks so that they could begin training together. He wanted them to assemble on a Saturday

159

evening, talk about planning over a few beers, then work out at Twickenham the following morning. He was determined to cut out the possibility of players treating Twickenham as an away match because they did not know the stadium well enough.

He said that fitness levels had to rise to those of South African and New Zealand players, and these levels would become a target of players in the four divisions of England – North, Midlands, South West and London – and would be monitored.

Weston knew all about fighting for proper fitness. When he was aged seven and a pupil at Bow School, Durham, he ran into a cricket stump while playing tip and run and it went into his knee. He was not allowed to play for three years and much later he had an operation on the same knee. When he was fully restored he made sure that he could kick with equal strength off either foot, an attribute which served him well In 1967, on an England tour of Canada, Weston was offered $30,000 to place-kick for an American football franchise in Toronto. He was offered terms covering six months of the year. He was not tempted.

Green was retained as coach through to the World Cup. He stressed the importance of England introducing more mobility to their forward play before the World Cup. The English game saw the reinstatement of the divisional championship and the introduction of the John Smith Merit Tables for senior clubs.

London called Roger Uttley in as coach. Since retiring as a player he had had little involvement with the England team except for some occasional help at coaching sessions when Dick Greenwood was in charge. He was far from unhappy or inactive in rugby because of his job as director of physical education at Harrow School.

Uttley had to prepare the London team for just three matches. He said at the time: "My philosophy is that players have to accept more responsibility for what goes on on the field. You get the impression rightly or wrongly that at international level if the team fails blame is laid at coaches and selectors. That may be true to a degree but, if team selection has the support of the players, the players accept that the people off the field have done their bit and it is up to them to produce."

He believed that London had nothing to lose and that all the other teams expected to beat them. Further, he thought that the South West would do well and that there was a case for fielding the entire Bath team in South West colours. In the event, London beat the North and the South West and lost only to the Midlands, the eventual champions.

The divisional championship put more than 60 players into intense competition over three successive Saturdays. The Midlands, coached by Alan Davies and led by Neil Mantell, both of the Nottingham club, did not play an expansive game but won their matches convincingly.

This was 1985. That December eight of the players who would be in the England Grand Slam team of 1991 took part in the divisional championship – a definite indication that the selectors knew what they were doing.

CHAPTER 23

From January 1987 until May 1987 every leading player in the world had his mind focussed on the new target of the World Cup. Four pools were created for the 16 nations who were invited to the Cup. England were placed with Australia, Japan and the USA in a group based in Sydney and Brisbane. Scotland were in a group with France, Zimbabwe and Romania. Wales were placed with Ireland, Canada and Tonga. New Zealand, Fiji, Italy and Argentina were in the fourth pool.

The four home countries did not suddenly change courses to accommodate the new challenge. England and Wales each played eight full internationals in the 16-month build up. Scotland and Ireland played nine because they fulfilled fixtures with Romania; but everywhere the work rate grew and much of the emphasis in preparation went on away from public gaze.

England began the 1986 championship with Melville restored as captain, Colclough at lock after a year's absence and two new caps, Simon Halliday, the Bath centre who had been an under-23 player in 1982, and Graham Robbins, the Coventry No. 8.

Andrew's kicking was the dominant factor in the 21–18 win over Wales at Twickenham. After putting over six penalties he dropped a goal to win the match in the third minute of injury time. Jonathan Davies had set up the only try of the game in the second half with a scorching break but England considered they were worthy winners.

Events soon turned against them. With only one alteration, Harrison for the injured Underwood, England set off confidently for Murrayfield but the Scots and Gavin Hastings in particular took them apart in no uncertain terms. The 33–6 win was Scotland's largest in the history of the fixture, and Hastings played a major part with five penalties and three conversions in a 100 per cent kicking performance.

In the dressing room afterwards – the quietest, said Melville, that he had been in – Green addressed his players firmly and at length about what had happened and what lay ahead. "We are learning", said Melville, "that it is the faster and more athletic packs which are causing the trouble for us. Now everyone wants to play again to erase the memory of what happened against Scotland."

Not everyone was given the chance. England made changes all the way through the team with the exception of the half backs and the second row, and in particular introduced Dean Richards of Leicester at No. 8. Richards had been close to selection for some time and, when he was finally admitted, England had chosen a player who was to become one of the most influential figures of the eighties and beyond.

Richards had played for England Schools as a lock forward and for the under-23 team at No. 8. He might reasonably have been chosen a couple of years earlier, because at every ground where Richards played at the time he seemed to leave an indelible impression of his skill and strength. Off the pitch, however, Richards would give no hints of his skill. He was unbelievably modest, and remains so, but has maintained such high standards that in the broad canvas of English rugby he has to be regarded as something of a one-off.

Richards began against Ireland at Twickenham on a bone-hard pitch, the result of severe frost. He touched down one pushover try after three minutes of the second half and another with three minutes left and came off to instant congratulations from the referee, Clive Norling of Wales, and the adulation of supporters who thronged round him later, providing the biggest obstacle of the day. England won 25–20.

Finally, England travelled to Paris but fell behind 0–17 early in the second half and were comprehensively outplayed by the brisker French backs. England lost Melville in the first half, with the obvious inference that injuries were going to continue to bedevil his time at the top, and were all too often on the back foot. France won 29–10, to share the championship with Scotland.

England then flew out to Australia to play in the inaugural New South Wales international seven-a-side tournament at the new Concord Oval a few miles from the centre of Sydney. As this ground was going to be used for the World Cup matches in Sydney the following year it was a chance for some of the players to check out the facilities – but England missed an opportunity to make an impact.

In their first match England were beaten 6–24 by Spain, not a result to be proud of, they lost by the same score to Australia and only just beat the Netherlands. This meant that England did not qualify for the quarter-finals and the captain, Andy Ripley, then 38, admitted: "One can grapple around for excuses but basically we weren't good enough on the day. We took Spain too casually."

Wales, with Jonathan Davies in mercurial form, beat New Zealand in the preliminaries of the event, but the All Blacks went on to thrash Australia 32–0 in the final. Of the England squad Kevin Simms, Fran Clough, Peter Williams, Richard Hill and Peter Winterbottom were to return to the ground the following year for the World Cup. However, Concord Oval began as a ground where England did not achieve their best, and it remained that way for subsequent visits.

Next, with little more than a year left before the World Cup, a team containing players from France, New Zealand, Australia and South Africa defeated the British Lions, led by Colin Deans of Scotland, 15–7 at Cardiff – and once more emphasized the gap between north and south of the equator.

Meanwhile Mike Weston was seeing the results of some of his ideas on how the England squad could be made to feel more important. On a personal basis, the players were offered a larger allocation of tickets to matches, their wives and girlfriends were incorporated into international weekends, a scheme was set up for dental and physiotherapy treatment for players, and they were supplied with formal and leisure clothing.

Weston had noted that France warmed up for matches in Paris by working at an indoor training area at the Parc des Princes. At his suggestion a scrummaging machine was installed at Twickenham for the England pack to use. Before the summer of 1986 was over, Weston and his co-selectors – Green, Des Seabrook and Tony Jorden – had chosen a squad of 45 players to begin training for the World Cup. Yet even in so large a squad four players who were eventual Cup selections were not included.

An indication of England's planning for 1987 came with the selection of the team against Japan in October 1986. England showed their hand in a good many positions, with up to nine players destined to stay as first choices into the following year. Hill, then 25, was appointed captain for the first time.

England beat Japan 39–12 and chose another squad to travel to Portugal for warm-weather training. A specialist training camp at Acoteias on the Algarve was the destination of the squad, which was again led by Hill, for the four-day trip.

It was here, among the pine trees, on the long, golden beaches, and on the training track that the significant change in England's approach was put on view. The players were advised how to run by Tom McNab, the former AAA national coach. All aspects of their fitness were checked, against the clock where necessary, with the promise that they would be checked again at regular intervals.

England also had a game against a Portugal team. This was played on an unpretentious arena hastily converted from a soccer pitch in a nearby town and England scored eleven tries in defeating some very raw opposition 62–15. Green was delighted with the effort put into training and the skills displayed in the match. "We have worked harder than any other England team," was his assessment.

The squad came home from Portugal knowing that they would return. Each one knew, as well, that the countdown to the World Cup was intensifying. Will Carling, who was not in that squad, was also aware of the prospect of Cup selection because he had now begun to claim attention on a higher stage than ever before.

At Durham University Carling came into contact with Ted Wood, latterly the bursar to the college of St Hilda and St Bede, a man who had played rugby until he was 32 and who had begun coaching with the Huddersfield club in 1969. Five years later he started to coach at Durham and the University grew in stature as a rugby establishment, producing more than a dozen players who went on to play for England.

Wood, in harness with Peter Dixon, an England flanker, produced some consistent University teams from the 4,000 students in residence. He also had two years as coach to England Students; among others, Carling, Chris Oti, Rory Underwood, Jon Webb and Fran Clough passed through his hands.

Wood had seen Carling as a schoolboy and had encouraged him to go to Durham. In his first year, Carling was chosen for the university at full back, but in 1986 he played as a replacement for Durham City at Boroughmuir and that brief evidence earned him selection for Durham county. Carling was amazed with his selection, yet that same year he was also selected for the North in the 1986 divisional championship.

The North won the championship at a canter and Carling was one of their eye-catching players. In the 34–6 win against London which gave the North the title with an unbeaten record, Carling's running and passing justified everything which had been said about him in his earlier years. He was so good that his inexperience at this level did not show.

Wood, who was to move on to manage the North the following year in succession to Geoff Cooke, described himself as a "paid-up member of the Carling fan club". Wood might have considered Carling as a possibility for the World Cup. Carling himself understood that the selectors would not choose him in the 1987 championship but that a Cup place was a serious option.

Much later, when the World Cup squad was finalized, Carling was not in it and heard through the grapevine that he was not included because he was considered too tired. He had continued with his studies, he had commuted to London to train and play for Harlequins, and suddenly a prize which dangled ahead of him was taken away. The three centres chosen were Jamie Salmon, Kevin Simms and Fran Clough. This surprised Salmon because he had been under the impression that Carling would be one of the trio. Will Carling and Mike Weston, as far as can be assessed, did not have a conversation together for some time afterwards.

CHAPTER 24

The 1987 championship went to France with no argument whatsoever. Not only did they win the championship, they took the Grand Slam, their fourth. The only team which headed them was Ireland who led 10–0 in the final French game before being overhauled 19–13.

England held a trial before the championship and squeezed home against the Rest 10–9. The Rest, captained by Harrison, included Carling at centre. Afterwards Maurice Colclough announced that he would no longer be available for international football. As Steve Bainbridge was injured and Dooley was recovering from a knee operation, England were suddenly short of experienced locks.

The first match should have been against Scotland in January, but Twickenham was covered in snow, making the terraces and walkways unsafe even if the pitch were playable, and the Scottish borders were also hit by bad weather, making it virtually impossible for the Scotland team to assemble on time. So Dudley Wood, who had succeeded Bob Weighill as secretary of the Rugby Football Union, had the unenviable job of calling off the first championship match under his jurisdiction.

This meant that England began in Dublin and in a match in which Ireland, in the words of their captain Donal Lenihan, reverted to the traditional Irish game of "spoiling and messing", England were seen off 17–0. England were ill-prepared for the wet and slippery conditions, and the absence from the England pack of men who knew the business was damaging.

A more concerted effort was produced against France, with Dooley and Bainbridge back in harness at lock, and with three penalties from Rose and a dropped goal by Andrew, England led 12–3 at half-time. However, when France hit their stride and began to launch their flankers and centres at pace towards the England defences, the match turned and it was a try by Sella after a 65-yard sprint which changed the outcome. France won 19–15.

Green's assessment of the England performance was that they had picked up some of the pieces and now had something to build on. "This team is good enough to win in Cardiff," he declared.

The Wales–England match was even more critical than usual. The two countries knew that a fairly predictable set of circumstances could lead to them playing in the quarter-finals of the World Cup three months ahead and this added to the tensions associated with the fixture.

Both sides were undoubtedly steamed up, England possibly more so than Wales. Wales kicked off, in wind and rain, and in the first line-out there were some verbal exchanges among the forwards and then fighting broke out. It took time for the referee, Ray Megson of Scotland, to restore order and when this was done Phil Davies, the Welsh No. 8 who had been hit by Dooley, went off with a facial injury which later proved to be a fractured cheekbone.

This laid a foundation of bad feeling which never really dispersed despite frequent warnings by the referee and a stream of penalties, nearly twice as many against England as against Wales. Inevitably penalties played a major part in the scoring and Mark Wyatt kicked five for Wales and Rose four for England. Jonathan Davies set up Stuart Evans to score the only try and Wales won 19–12.

The bitterness lived on because Wales put the blame for the day's difficulties firmly on England's shoulders. "The bonus for us," said Tony Gray, the Welsh coach, "was the way we maintained our discipline. What happened there is England's problem, not ours." Hill, whose third championship match as captain had brought a third defeat, said that the players knew each other so well that there were bound to be one-to-one confrontations.

The Rugby Union shared the views aired on the day that England were at fault. Four players were suspended for one match – Hill, Chilcott, Dawe and Dooley – and all that was left to play for was a face-saving match against Scotland and the chance to build a modicum of confidence before the World Cup.

In Hill's enforced absence, England suddenly needed a captain and there were not many candidates to take on the job of leading the side against a Scotland team which was in search of a victory to complete a Triple Crown.

Harrison, on the right wing, was the choice. He had eight caps at the time and was captain of Yorkshire. He had an impressive athletics background as a sprinter and triple-jumper and made his first mark as a rugby player as a school-boy scrum-half. After a road accident in 1975 he was advised not to play again and did not do so for two years, but in 1978 he joined Wakefield and slowly progressed to the England team.

Richards played his first match of the championship, having recovered from injury. The other alterations caused by England's disciplinary measures brought Harding in at scrum-half, Nigel Redman at lock, Paul Rendall at prop and Brian Moore at hooker. This was Moore's first match – he had been understudy to Dawe through the championship – and introduced to the England team a lively mind (he was a law graduate from Nottingham University), a vociferous talker and a hugely competitive player who seemed to regard the top stratum of the game as a jumping-off point for even greater things. He was ambition unlimited.

One other player was introduced – fly-half Peter Williams of Orrell. He was then 28 and had been playing for Lancashire for eight years. England had tried him in different teams from under-23 level onwards, and just before winning his first cap Williams had been fly-half in an England "B" team which beat France at Bath. He had had experience in South Africa, playing for the Transvaal side, and also in Australia. His selection meant that Andrew, who had mostly been first choice for three years, was dropped.

All these alterations in personnel and attitude produced a rebound performance by England, whose scoring was dominated by Rose. A penalty try was awarded, after Harrison had been obstructed, and Rose scored one himself in the second half from his own high kick. Rose scored 17 points, England won 21–12, and from a messy season which left England joint bottom of the championship with Wales all kinds of encouragement had emerged.

With the exception of Halliday, who was not available, the England team which beat Scotland was chosen in its entirety to move on to the World Cup. The players who had been disciplined were also reinstated. The squad read in full:

Full backs	– Marcus Rose (Harlequins), Jon Webb (Bristol)
Wings	– Mike Harrison (Wakefield, capt.), Rory Underwood (Leicester), Mark Bailey (Wasps)
Centres	– Jamie Salmon (Harlequins), Kevin Simms (Wasps), Fran Clough (Orrell)
Half-backs	– Peter Williams (Orrell), Rob Andrew (Wasps), Richard Hill (Bath), Richard Harding (Bristol)
Front row	– Jeff Probyn (Wasps), Paul Rendall (Wasps), Gary Pearce (Northampton), Gareth Chilcott (Bath), Brian Moore (Nottingham), Graham Dawe (Bath)

171

Second row   – Wade Dooley (Fylde), Steve Bainbridge
             (Fylde), Nigel Redman (Bath)

Back row   – Dean Richards (Leicester), David Egerton
             (Bath), Peter Winterbottom (Headingley),
             Jon Hall (Bath), Gary Rees (Nottingham)

The die was cast; Carling, who had been hopeful, was
not required. Through most of that winter he had been
commuting from Durham to play with Harlequins, a nursery
for many England players and the club of several England
captains. Dick Best, the Harlequins coach, would meet him
from the train at Kings Cross station and take him to training,
then drive him back to Kings Cross so that Carling could
catch the night sleeper back to the north-east. Carling missed
out . . . but in terms of the England team he did not have that
much longer to wait.

CHAPTER 25

Mike Weston, along with all the other World Cup managers, had toured the match venues in Australia and New Zealand. Six months ahead of the competition he was not happy with the hotel accommodation which was being proposed and described the playing surface on the ground where England would play all three of their pool matches as "appalling". Nearer to the actual competition England had been assured that they would be given the largest hotel rooms available and that the playing pitch had improved considerably.

It was almost a year since the intensive fitness work for the World Cup had begun. Using basic athletic tests Tom McNab's first impression was that there was little ongoing fitness training by most of the players off season. In tests the England backs all scored highly, not just in speed and bounding, but also in weights and shot throwing. Rory Underwood threw the shot at world-class level, only 50cm shorter than the Olympic decathlon champion Daley Thompson. Props came out poorly in almost every test of athleticism but the hookers were impressive.

McNab reasoned that few players had any concept of the elements of warm-up and few had any ideas of the specific fitness requirements of their positon. He established an educational programme to teach the players a vocabulary of exercise while also building a basic fitness platform for the coming season.

McNab pinpointed the fitness specifics for each position – accelerative speed for a scrum half, absolute speed for a wing, fast-striding repetition with short recoveries for a loose forward, explosive power in the legs for the second row and upper-body strength in the front row to enable players to fix their scrum positions. Ideally, said McNab, all players must be fast, strong over short distances, powerful in the upper body in order to tackle and maul, and possessed of the ability to recover quickly from high levels of effort.

McNab reckoned that the first training camp in Portugal was a major breakthrough because it showed players the levels of training which they could achieve, working in the best possible conditions. By the time of a second visit to Portugal just before the Cup began, McNab knew that England were in superb condition.

On 12 May England flew out to Australia in order to play their first match against the home team on 23 May. In between they settled in at Rushcutter's Bay to the south of Sydney Harbour and on the road to Bondi Beach. A training ground was situated immediately to the rear of their hotel.

It was in training that England suffered their first blow when Bainbridge pulled up in a sprint session and was ruled out of the opening game. Redman played instead.

The World Cup burst into action in New Zealand but attracted less attention in Sydney where Australia, the co-favourites, drew a gate of just under 18,000 for the opener against England. Maybe the new venue instead of the old favourite, the Sydney Cricket Ground, had something to do with it. Maybe the World Cup just did not grip the Sydney public from start to finish. Whatever the reason, there was room enough in the ground when Australia kicked off – and within two minutes England had lost Rose at full back, knocked out as he came into the line. He was eventually taken off on a stretcher – and out of the competition. Webb, the reserve full back, thus gained his first cap.

England were well in the match at 6–6 early in the second half, Harrison having scored a try in the corner, when Australia were granted a try by the referee, Keith Lawrence, which everyone except him knew was not a try. David Campese, the Australian wing, was awarded a touch-down in spite of the fact that he had lost the ball going over the line. England did not let their heads drop as a result but the game had gone away from them, and the final score was 19–6 to Australia.

England next beat Japan 60–7, having taken a few days away from Sydney at Hamilton Island off the Queensland coast, and then beat the USA 34–6 to reach the quarter finals where the line up was: Australia v. Ireland; France v. Fiji; New Zealand v. Scotland; England v. Wales. It was ironic that two of the home countries should have to meet so far from home in such a crucial competition with sudden death the only option. As Green said: "I just hope my coaching career and that of Tony Gray of Wales will not be dependent on a quarter-final result in Australia."

Scotland were the first to go, beaten 3–30 by New Zealand. "There was no way we could stem their support play. We have played three games in seven days and maybe we just ran out of steam in the finish," said Derrick Grant, the Scottish coach. Ireland followed, beaten 33–15 by Australia.

England and Wales met on a Monday afternoon in Brisbane. England chose the team which finished the match against Australia but Wales were known to have doubts about the fitness of their key lock forward, Bob Norster, and fly-half Jonathan Davies.

It was quickly evident that Norster had next to no mobility and that Davies was limping; but Norster was still able to frustrate England in the line-out, as he did throughout his career, and it was an injury to the England loose-head prop Rendall which actually led to a decisive score.

Rendall came off after 27 minutes because a finger had scratched his eyeball. England did not put a replacement on for the next scrum, which just happened to be a defensive one close to their line. The ball squeezed out of the side of that scrum and Gareth Roberts, the Welsh flanker, seized on it to score. The important first blow had been struck by Wales. They scored two more tries to win 16–3, and for England the World Cup was over.

While Welsh elation could be felt all over Brisbane that evening, glum solitude settled over the England camp. A few players went out to train, others sat analysing what had gone wrong. They had trained and worked as never before, including a three-hour session on the eve of the match which was later judged to have been too long, and still they could not nail Wales. After all, Brisbane was not Cardiff.

The next morning Weston, Green and Harrison held a conference in Weston's suite in the Park Royal Hotel, Brisbane, overlooking the botanical gardens. The mood was sombre but realistic. "We realized our shortcoming a year ago," said Weston, "and tried to do something about it. Now our time is up but maybe we have set the ball rolling. We are hoping to get the structure altered and I would like to think this will be followed up."

The semi-finals were set with Australia playing France in a compelling match which drew only 17,768 spectators to the Concord Oval and which was won by France 30–24 in the fifth minute of injury time with a stunning try by Blanco. The next day in Brisbane New Zealand destroyed Wales 49–6.

Australia had to leave home for the first time for the third-place match against Wales in Rotorua, New Zealand. Neither side seemed enthusiastic, initially, on having to play at all, but there was a vibrant atmosphere at Rotorua, as there was at all World Cup venues in New Zealand, and Wales had much more vocal support than they anticipated. Australia had their flanker, David Codey, sent off after only four minutes and the match stayed alive until the fifth minute of injury time when Paul Thorburn, with a conversion from touch, gave Wales victory by 22–21.

As for the final, maybe France had left too much of their

176

best for the win over Australia and were never truly in contention against the All Blacks in Auckland. New Zealand, led from scrum-half by David Kirk, won 29–9 with three tries against one, and nobody would have argued that the best side had won the first competition for the Webb Ellis Cup. Kirk, in a touching gesture, made sure that Andy Dalton, who was appointed captain of New Zealand but could not play because of injury, shared immediately in the victory celebrations.

The World Cup had arrived and was clearly here to stay. All across New Zealand it had been a predictable success, but less so in Australia where rugby union has to fight harder for its share of the market place. One of the recommendations after the event was that in future the World Cup should be staged in one country only. This was taken so seriously that when the 1991 World Cup was finalized it was agreed to stage it in England, Wales, Ireland, Scotland and France. This messy compromise between five nations negated the decision taken after the 1987 competition that either the four Home Unions should stage the 1991 cup or France alone should host it. Their fragmentation was obvious and should have been avoided.

CHAPTER 26

The journey from Australia to London, which began the day after England's defeat by Wales, was the start of the inquest into England's performance – or under-performance – in the quarter-final. As Paul Rendall nursed his sore eye he had real cause to curse the result against Wales because, if there were two things in rugby he truly enjoyed, one was playing against Wales and the other was beating them. Six times he had experience of the former but had only two wins, both at Twickenham, and it was cruel that one of the long-term servants of the England front row should have been stood down not long before the 1991 win at Cardiff.

Rendall was one of 19 players, out of the 28 who eventually formed the World Cup squad, who needed treatment for injury during the competition. The back-up team of physio-therapist Kevin Murphy and doctor Ben Gilfeather was continuously active. More than 200 treatments were carried out in the time England were in Australia. In the first two weeks there were 70 treatments – in the last 12 days 146. As players were being asked to play international rugby much more often than the once-every-two-weeks cycle of the five nations' championship, this was not surprising.

England lost two players during the competition. Rose was hurt in the first match and Hall did not play because of a knee injury and went home. Huw Davies, who was on tour in Australia with Middlesex, replaced Rose and Micky Skinner, a gregarious Geordie who played in the back row for Harlequins, was brought out from England after an announcement on BBC television that his country needed him! Skinner, along with Jeff Probyn and David Egerton, was not asked to play in any of the four matches.

In the analysis which followed, there was plenty of intensive questioning of what England had done in the World Cup and what should be done next. Green, as coach, believed that England's pattern of preparation was an effective structure which could act as a model for the future. That proved to be an accurate assessment.

He also said that physical conditioning should become a permanent feature of the preparation for international football, with the content increasingly fed through to other levels in the game. Green further believed that England had made important developments in style before and during the World Cup and these needed to be taken further. He thought, too, that the squad with which he had worked was now better equipped to cope with international rugby than a year earlier.

Weston was as disappointed as everyone else at the quarter-final defeat, but also stressed that not everything which had been established should be thrown away because of it. He believed that the foundations had been laid and that the whole playing structure of English rugby at the top was falling into place. The final piece in the jigsaw was the establishment of club leagues under the banner of the Courage clubs championship at the start of the 1987–8 season.

Unfortunately, time was ticking away for Weston and Green. What nagged at Weston was that England might have had one big training session too many – on the eve of the Welsh game – while the Welsh team spent the day on the beach. Looking back, he felt there was mental and physical tiredness that day in Brisbane, not helped by a wet pitch. However, he stressed: "If there is anyone to blame, I'm as much to blame as anyone else."

179

Both Weston and Green made it clear that they would like another year with the squad. When Weston learned that the Rugby Union did not want to continue with Green as coach he suggested that Green became a selector and form a panel of three – Weston, Green and Jorden. The coaches, he went on, should be Roger Uttley and Alan Davies.

During 1987 Weston estimated that he had been attending to his business affairs, which included an estate agency in Durham that he had founded 25 years before and become its principal, for an average of only two days a week. He foresaw that the structure of the estate agency business was about to undergo change, and some of his friends were advising him that he should either carry on with the rugby job full time and give up the business or resign from rugby to concentrate on the business – but not do both.

"We all wanted one more year with England," says Weston, "because we felt frustrated that all we had done had not come to fruition. It was all there waiting to happen if we carried on on the same lines. The players were happy – in a period of 18 months to two years there had been more changes in the set up for them than there had been in the previous 30 years."

While Weston argued his case with the Rugby Union he learned of a proposal that he should remain as manager and sole selector until the end of 1987 (there was no autumn international that year). He felt that was farcical because he had built a good team of people to run England rugby. At the same time his business advisers were still telling him not to remain involved in rugby. So Weston took the decision to resign.

A few weeks passed by. Then, one evening, Geoff Cooke took a telephone call in his home. The caller was the chairman of the Rugby Union coaching sub-committee, Danie Serfontein (a dentist who just happened to have Weston as one of his patients). Serfontein said he had something to discuss with Cooke which could not be done on the telephone. They agreed to meet a couple of days later at the Scotch Corner

180

Hotel on the Great North Road, geographically convenient for both of them.

There was an interesting contrast in how two men who held such responsible positions in England rugby learned of their fate in 1987. When Weston discovered the grand plan for the game involved him as sole selector he had just attended a garden party at Buckingham Palace. Now Cooke set out to drive to his meeting with Serfontein wondering what on earth it was all about and surmising that he was going to be asked to be a selector.

At the time, Cooke was 46. He is a Cumbrian who went to Carlisle Grammar School and then to St John's, York, to study physical education. He had been a midfield player with Bradford and with Cumberland and Westmorland and had captained both teams. He had coached Bradford, Yorkshire and the Northern division. When Serfontein asked to see him, Cooke was working as principal sports development officer for Leeds City Council.

"I was quite staggered when we actually met because Danie came straight out with it," says Cooke. "He told me that Mike Weston had resigned and would I take over, how did I feel about it, was it possible. It really went from there. I was obviously pleased and somewhat surprised because I had not even been an England selector. I had contributed, but nothing more. I talked over the implications with Danie. I was delighted and wanted to accept but obviously the immediate consideration was my work and I said that I would have to speak to my employers. I also wanted to talk to my wife Sue because of the implications of the change in our lifestyle. So I asked for 24 hours before I gave my final answer."

Cooke's employers were sympathetic and supportive and so was his wife who stressed that he would only have one such chance in his life. The initial appointment was for one year, and in the two-week period before the official announcement was made Cooke was asked to think about which people he wanted to work with him.

He made it clear from the start that he wanted to be involved as a tracksuit manager instead of one who was concerned more obviously with administration. That was accepted. Next he appointed John Elliott, the former Nottingham hooker, as a co-selector, and that was ratified almost immediately by the Rugby Union. The appointment of coach was deferred because the Rugby Union had already decided that this would be done in December, after the divisional championship. Cooke gave the name of the coach he wanted and he was given approval to sound him out and find out if he was available. Roger Uttley said he was.

The first task of the new management team was to select sides for a trial at Twickenham in January 1988. Cooke has not staged a trial since but because of his newness he agreed to a trial at that stage. He was also aware that the work which Weston had done had been worthwhile and had gone a long way towards professionalising the England approach. However, he was critical of the playing standards of the squad. "We felt that we had players capable of winning set-piece ball but not very good at keeping it and that England were poor in their concept of how to play the game and make effective use of the ball. I did not like the style of play which was set-piece and kick-orientated and characterized by fear of failure. We saw our first task as raising the level of confidence to create a more open and trusting environment, to change the attitude to playing international rugby, to establish what was possible and necessary in terms of commitment."

Cooke set up a squad session at Worcester so that he could introduce himself and his lines of thinking to the players. As part of that day Cooke sat with a small group of established players and asked them for their views of the situation. He wanted to know what they thought of the set-up and what irritated them or pleased them. Cooke took the squad in a training period as well and observed them at work under Don Rutherford and Chalkie White.

Changes began to appear in the squad as Cooke made his

assessments and travelled the road, looking at players, in a hectic period of acclimatization. He felt it was important he was seen around the grounds of England ("Up and down the country people were saying 'Geoff Who?'") because nearly all his previous involvement had been in the North. He found himself going to grounds he had never visited before and introducing himself to all kinds of people – and began to have the first feelings of the loneliness which might accompany the job.

"Up to then I hadn't done anything wrong because I hadn't done anything," he says. "People generally went out of their way to talk to me and there were no axes to grind at that stage. It was almost like a honeymoon period because there was quite a lot of attention, people were talking to me, and it was easy because we hadn't put our heads on the block. It was only when you come to pick your first team, and we had some injuries which affected preconceived ideas, that things changed."

CHAPTER 27

The North won all their matches in taking the divisional championship in 1987 and Carling was again one of their outstanding players. In the trial which followed on 2 January Carling and Kevin Simms were promoted to the senior side because of injuries but the "A" team was beaten by the "B" team 13–7.

Cooke quickly announced his first England team for the match against France in Paris. There were three new caps – Carling at centre, Probyn at prop and Skinner at flanker.

Nobody needed to tell the exuberant Skinner how to perform and equally there was no need to advise Probyn on what to expect at tight-head prop because he was aged 30 and knew the business. As for Carling, there appeared to be no problems either. Les Cusworth, the England fly-half that day, spent some time before the game studying Carling's reaction to his debut and decided that he was totally ready for it.

The match started promisingly for England and for Carling. He put in a diagonal thrust at great pace but did not time his pass properly and with two players outside him the move died unprofitably. However, the England forwards were confident and kept pressure on France all the way through the first half and well into the second, so that with 16 minutes left England were ahead 9–3.

France then turned the game with two scores in the final nine minutes, a try by their No. 8 Laurent Rodriguez settling it when he picked up the ball after Harrison, the England captain, had been unable to control it. France won 10–9.

England had gone to Paris with a great deal of doom and gloom about their prospects. Some had anticipated a defeat by 20 or 30 points but England outplayed France in many areas and simply put down too many chances to be sure of winning.

Carling was now a full international and went to the French banquet wearing a multi-coloured bow tie and a wide grin. He had carefully packed away his first England shirt and reasoned that, as England had been expecting a hammering at the Parc des Princes, the result was not too bad. He also realized that his first international had sped by so quickly that he was hard pressed to analyze what had happened.

Against Wales at Twickenham England suffered in different if predictable ways because Robert Norster continued his dominance of the line-out and Jonathan Davies, one of four fly-halves who were chosen for the Welsh backs that day, created his usual amount of havoc. Only a brilliant recovery tackle by Jon Webb, after Davies had sold him a dummy, prevented England going a score down late in the first half.

Wales took over in the second half with Adrian Hadley scoring two tries, one after Tony Clement had counter-attacked from full back, the other after one of those searing breaks by Davies, and Wales won 11–3. "We made some howling mistakes," said Cooke. "We played our first two games, with a new management team, and lost them both. You're heading for potential disaster and you hear the supporters saying that you are going to be as bad as the other lot were. All this is coming at you from different angles and this was the first sign of the enormity of what you're involved in. It hits you, all this huge interest of all these people who look to England to satisfy their own pride. Suddenly you are faced with a potential season of whitewash."

Cooke had to telephone Harrison, the captain, to tell him

he was out following the Wales game. He had known Harrison for years with Yorkshire and the North, and it was probably through Cooke's pushing and support that Harrison had made the England team in the first place. Cooke never liked telling players they were dropped but says: "I hope I never shirk from it. I'm the guy that has to do the nasty part."

Chris Oti effectively replaced Harrison because he was the new wing, on the left, with Underwood switching to the right. Oti had scored two tries for Cambridge in the Varsity match two months earlier and his reputation as a player uncommonly difficult to halt was growing week by week.

England's next game was against Scotland. Andrew and Halliday were chosen at fly-half and centre, Melville resumed the captaincy, and the England pack stayed as it was. They were hardly favourites for the journey to Murrayfield: England had been beaten in their previous 14 away games.

Anyone who thought that Oti's involvement was going to lead to a feast of running by England was in for a disappointment. There was little open football and no scoring at all in the first half, with Gavin Hastings missing four penalty attempts and Webb three. In the second half Andrew dropped a goal and Webb kicked two penalties for England to win 9–6.

The England performance was not viewed with any pleasure by Derrick Grant in his last match as coach of Scotland. He accepted that England came to do a job, but at a cost. He accused England of killing the game dead and of planning to slow the match down by whatever means possible.

Cooke's response was that both he and Roger Uttley were "totally flabbergasted. Scotland took the defeat very, very badly. It was something that surprised us and took us back a little. We didn't think we had provoked anything. It was an awful game from a spectator's point of view but we were delighted to win. It was a major result for us and from that point things started to pick up. We then felt we were able to get moving a bit."

Later that night, Melville too defended his team. "We went out to do a job on a ground where it has become increasingly difficult to win. We played to the conditions and we were determined not to let Scotland gain control. That is why we won, and I promise that we will build on this for our final match against Ireland."

Cooke and the England squad now headed for the final match of the championship – a game which cost them the services of Melville for ever but which allowed England to play the sort of football the manager had hoped for. He was already tired of people telling him that it was no use expecting England to play in the way his Yorkshire and North teams had done; the Ireland match vindicated his beliefs.

England's 35–3 win brought six tries, confirmed a breakthrough in playing style, convinced Cooke that this type of football was possible on a regular basis and left him devastated by what had happened to Melville. Cooke had played against Melville's father and had known the young player since he was an aspiring teenager.

The day after Melville had been carried off, Cooke visited him in hospital. The thought that he had to find another captain did not then cross his mind, but it soon did.

As already recorded, that season England played Ireland once more, winning the Dublin Millenium game 21–10. It was then a matter of preparing for a tour to Australia and Fiji. Of the England management team, only Cooke was available and he was placed in charge of team strategy and the backs. Alan Davies, the Midlands coach, was put in charge of conditioning, and David Robinson, the North coach, was given the task of running the forwards.

Halliday, the one player who had been unable to travel to the World Cup the previous year, was able to go to Australia for part of the tour only. Carling was sitting examinations at Durham and it was decided that Halliday would have the first section of the tour, Carling the second.

Carling wound up his last English season as a student by playing for the Army (as his scholarship to Durham allowed

187

him to do) against the Royal Air Force at Twickenham, then moving on to the John Player Special Cup final on behalf of Harlequins against Bristol.

This final, the 17th, helped put the Cup on the map. It attracted a record crowd for the time of 37,000 and Quins became the first London club to win the Cup with such a commitment to running and attacking that they caught Bristol off balance.

Quins scored three tries in their 28–22 win and Carling had two of them. Both moves began with counter-attacks by Quins and some fine running resulted. Carling's second try, for example, ended a move of 75 yards. As he said: "We did them for pace. We decided that if we got early ball we would run at them and we caught them cold."

One of the prominent players for Quins in the final was Paul Ackford, the lock forward, who was in his first season with the club. Ackford, then 30, had done something of a disappearing act since playing for England "B" in 1979, but this final proved he was definitely a contender again.

Ackford first played rugby at Plymouth College, then won a place in the Devon Schools side at No. 8. Next he went to Kent University to read English and joined the Rosslyn Park club. While he was still at university he was chosen for Devon, then for the South West against New Zealand.

In 1979 he won a blue at Cambridge and took up teaching at Dulwich College. Next he joined the Metropolitan Police, at the age of 25, and has now reached the rank of inspector. Ackford played rugby for the police as well – without making any notable impression – and he was almost out of time when he decided to make one more bid for recognition at the top of the game.

Ackford was lucky. His one last try brought him into contact with Dick Best, the Harlequins coach, who said that he need not bother to turn up at the club unless he was totally committed to reaching the top. This is the sort of comment which Best makes when he is trying to assess a player's level of interest and of course it usually provokes a reaction.

188

Ackford dug in and worked and when he had reached one peak he decided to go for another. Best, rarely showing pleasure or praise at Ackford's achievements, kept chipping away because he could see the potential of the giant policeman. The Cup final, with Ackford winning line-out possession and working effectively in the running game, showed him as a magnificent prospect.

Indeed, if Geoff Cooke had delayed his selection of the tour party to Australia until after that final, Ackford would surely have gone.

CHAPTER 28

England departed for Australia in the knowledge that no previous English side had ever won a Test there. Yet confidence was solid after the two victories over Ireland, and as the squad settled in at the Ko Huna village resort outside the Queensland sugar town of Mackay hopes were high.

Starting a tour in the warmth of Queensland quickly proved to England that the demands of the climate in Australia have to be taken fully into account, and by the time they had played three matches in the Sunshine State the players began to understand why people often kept their cut flowers in the fridge before putting them on display.

Orwin was probably aware that England had no long-term plan for him as captain, but he took on the task with all the commitment to be expected from a player who had lengthy experience with Gloucester and Bedford, among others, and warned from the outset that it could be a difficult trip. He stressed after the second game: "Things aren't going to happen just because we are out here. We have to work hard."

England were keeping half an eye on Wales, who were on tour at the same time in New Zealand, and noted that the Welsh were not settling too well either, losing two of their three matches before the first Test. A good many New Zealanders, including Wayne Shelford, captain of the All Blacks, believed that Wales were "a little bit slow round the track", and some of the Australians were beginning to say the same thing about England.

Wales were totally demolished 3–52 in their opening international in Christchurch, but the next day in Brisbane England pulled away to a promising start against Australia with two tries in a six-minute spell, scored by Underwood and John Bentley, the Sale wing, after lengthy runs. England had established a lead of 13–3 after 22 minutes but were then punished in the set pieces by the Australian forwards and were eventually overtaken, principally through Michael Lynagh's goal kicking, with 15 minutes left. Australia won 22–16.

Two more big games had still to be faced at the Concord Oval in Sydney and both were lost. New South Wales beat them 23–12 and 15 of their points came from a versatile ball-player named Brian Smith at fly-half, who was to forge a unique career by playing for Australia, Ireland, Oxford University and Leicester before tearing up his amateur status six months ahead of the 1991 World Cup to join a Rugby League club in Sydney.

The following weekend Wales, who had had to bring out six replacements during their tour, lost the second Test to the All Blacks by a record 9–54 and even though there were considerably improved contributions from many of the Welsh players, especially Jonathan Davies, who was captain for the day, it was still a numbing defeat.

Back in Sydney, Australia's new coach Bob Dwyer decided to field an altered pack for the second Test. England had the same options and Orwin's place must have been under threat from Nigel Redman; however, the only change in the pack meant a debut for the Bath flanker Andy Robinson.

Once more England were able to claim the lead with a try by Underwood but Australia's belief that they had the measure of the England side was quickly translated into points. Australia scored four tries and at times looked like running away with the game; only England's grim determination kept the eventual margin down to 28–8.

191

Once the Test series was lost, Cooke said all the correct things – England were disappointed, made too many errors and did not take their chances – but what was running through his mind were the comments on England's style of play from Australian coaches and officials.

"That was where the tour was beneficial because it taught us so many things," he said later. "It really showed us that we had to change our style and attitude, and in many ways it was a real turning point. It hadn't been a perfect set of circumstances because we did not have all the personnel we wanted and we did not play very well in a couple of games. But it helped to get it over to the players that our fitness and style were inappropriate to matches outside the five nations' championship such as we have just had. The Australians told me that they saw us as a side obsessed with set-piece play, that our style was stop-start and that we lurched from set piece to set piece, kicked aimlessly and tried to get penalties.

"I didn't resent what was said. I was irritated by it because it was totally contrary to what I believed I was trying to do, and what I thought we had made some progress in. Clearly, we hadn't. They said we had two types of player – the donkey, our forwards, who could win the ball at scrums and line-out but who just plodded around the field, and we had the backs who were quite skilful but without physical presence.

"That really helped to focus my mind and when I returned home I was determined to get these messages across – and with Australia coming back to play us so quickly after our return that gave us an ideal opportunity."

England had one more mission left on the tour, against Fiji in Suva. Webb, who had played full back in the two Tests in Australia, returned home to get married and Barnes, who had understudied Andrew at fly-half, was asked if he would play as Webb's replacement. Barnes declined and was chosen at fly-half with Andrew moving to full back. Orwin was withdrawn on fitness grounds and Harding led the side from scrum-half.

Suva lived up to its promise of providing sticky conditions.

There was a heavy storm ten minutes before the start and then the sun came out to raise the humidity. Until five minutes after half-time, with Fiji ahead 12–9, it was a tight contest but England then pulled ahead in a disciplined performance to score two tries through Underwood and let Barnes kick three goals to win 25–12. The Fijians were frustrated by the magnificent back-row play of Richards, Rees and Robinson – and very late in the day one Fijian was sent off for punching Rees. This allowed David Egerton to win a cap as a replacement in the eighth minute of injury time which was a record.

As the players flew home they were already aware that a 12-month programme for their development had been put into place. This involved fitness tests soon after their return, with further tests every two months, and more than a hundred players would be monitored. These tests were aimed at lifting fitness levels still higher than those achieved in 1987 – and anyone who wanted to remain in contention for England could not escape them.

Meanwhile Cooke set up a meeting of the coaches and chairmen of the four English divisions and reported on what had happened in Australia and how Australia viewed English rugby. It was decided that if Australia were to be beaten England, and the divisions, had to take the game to them by running it against them. Cooke considered it important that Best, the London coach, was totally on the same wavelength ... because London were Australia's first opponents.

Best assembled a comprehensively equipped London side and told them to go out and run. There were seven players from Harlequins in the team who had run to glory in the Cup final at the end of the previous season and they knew the mood which was required. London's 21–10 win was a torch-bearer for the English game with three tries, one from each of the wings, Mark Bailey and Andrew Harriman, to cement the victory.

Next the Australians played the North at Otley, taking a 9–0 lead, then Andrew took over the scoring with two penalties and a dropped goal before Dewi Morris, a scrum-half then with Liverpool St Helen's, topped off a fine display with a try from a tap penalty. The North won 15–9.

The South West were the last of the divisions to beat Nick Farr-Jones's Australians and recorded the highest margin, 26–10, at Bristol. The Midlands were the only side to miss out, beaten 18–25. But the pattern had been established which challenged England to beat Australia in the lone international on Guy Fawkes' Day, 1988.

The England side was set, with Carling as captain for the first time. The new caps, the Nigerian-born Harriman – who had a track time good enough to win a place in the 200 metres final of the Seoul Olympics that year, on the right wing – Ackford and Morris had all earned their places from their performances in the divisional games. The rest of the side had been in Australia and knew what was wanted.

The Australians had beefed up their resources by flying in Michael Lynagh, their goal kicking fly-half, after the tour had begun, and his presence added to the authority of the Australian backs. Australia led 9–3 after 20 minutes but Morris scored England's first try after a charge-down by Robinson to level the scores 9–9 at half-time.

David Campese then intercepted a pass from Webb to Halliday to run 70 yards and score. Then Underwood, who had scored two tries against the Wallabies in Australia, touched down twice in quick succession and England were on the way to a win by 28–19.

Carling laid the foundations for the last try, by Halliday, but then had to go off with concussion and was forced to miss the last moments of his first captaincy of the national side. Even so, he, and England, were on the way.

The Australians did not lose again on the tour. They swept through Scotland, winning the Test 32–13 at Murrayfield, and had a 40–22 win over the Barbarians at Cardiff. That made England feel even better.

CHAPTER 29

When in the summer of 1988 Carling graduated from Durham University, he decided not to progress into the Royal Regiment of Wales, as had been planned when he took an army scholarship. This decision meant that he had to go to the Royal Military Academy at Sandhurst to resign his commission. It was taken in close and private consultation with his family and refunding the Army would have cost several thousand pounds.

Carling did not want to miss playing regular first-class rugby for a season, which is what he believed his commitment to the Army would have meant. So he withdrew, a would-be soldier in an army family leaving for a civilian life. If he had stayed with the Army, Will Carling and Marcus Carling would have passed out together at Sandhurst.

As 1989 approached, the aspiring rugby player had two targets – to win the championship and go on the Lions tour to Australia. The coaches for that tour had been appointed early, with Ian McGeechan of Scotland and Roger Uttley of England gaining the vote. They had played together as Lions and now presented themselves as the obvious pairing for the tour which was to be the first to Australia alone. McGeechan was the senior coach.

A month before the championship England again went to Portugal and on the day before they returned Carling came

195

off a track session to run on grass and felt a pain in his left leg. That pain was to stay with him for six months, inhibiting his training for the championship. He had intensive treatment and medical care and managed to play all four games in the championship; but he found the effort of being captain for his first championship and being unable to play flat out a draining combination.

The other players knew of his problems and were supportive, so that Carling's play was not affected sufficiently for him to miss out on selection for the Lions. However, a month before the tour a specialist told him he would have to withdraw. Later in the summer when he was given clearance to train and subjected himself to some tests, he found that his left leg had 25 per cent less power compared to his right was one and a half inches slimmer.

Carling still made strides in his captaincy. He was asked to sit in on selection and to give his views on whether this player or that player would blend into the squad. However, if there was any actual voting to be done it was left to the three nominated selectors.

Recalling what he had heard his father say about running a platoon in the Army, Carling maintained contact with a hard-core group of about five players who he thought the most vocal and influential. If he thought a player needed to be spoken to he would do it. At the end of the season he was invited to a full committee meeting of the Rugby Union and asked questions on England's performance – another departure.

At the start of the championship there were two main issues: could England build on the form displayed against Australia and would Will Carling or Finlay Calder of Scotland be nominated captain of the Lions? The result of England's first match, which was against Scotland at Twickenham, helped the cause of Calder and reduced Carling's claims.

Scotland already had a match under their belts – a 23–7 win over Wales – while England suddenly realized that the

Australian win was a long time ago. So the Scots held something of an edge and confirmed it with the only try of the game, touched down by John Jeffrey following a high kick from their new fly-half from Melrose, Craig Chalmers.

Scotland led 12–6 early in the second half but England drew level with two penalties from Webb and the final score was a 12–12 draw. It was a scrappy game, strewn with penalties, and between them Webb and Andrew missed seven kicks at goal – one of them from 40 yards in injury time which would have won the day. However, as Calder said, it was a pretty poor display on both sides which stuttered about for 80 minutes. There was just too much tension.

Next England beat Ireland 16–3 in Dublin and some of the players who were to play crucial parts on the Lions tour – Moore, Ackford, Dooley, Richards and Teague – were outstanding; but everything paled before a thunderous performance against France at Twickenham which gave England an 11–0 win. This was raw stuff, full of driving forward power and discipline, and England beat the defending champions and recorded their first home win over France for ten years. England scored two tries, the first of them showing that even France were terrified of Oti's finishing powers and speed. Oti came on a diagonal run but his timing was off and the scissors with Carling did not take place. However, Oti had drawn three French defenders – and Carling retained the ball to run on and score.

Carling came off in disbelief – not with the England display, which also included a try by Andy Robinson in his greatest game for England, but because he could not come to terms with the fact that France had not scored at all. It had been 36 years since that had happened at Twickenham.

The last match of the championship was against Wales at Cardiff. A win for England would have given them the title and Wales did not sound much of a prospect because they had been beaten in all three games. The signs and noises from the England camp were indeed encouraging but Paul Thorburn, the Welsh captain, had assured me some weeks

197

earlier: "If there is anybody you don't lose to, it's England."

The side which had beaten France was retained. Wales packed in as much experience as they could find – Jonathan Davies had departed for Rugby League earlier in the season, to leave a huge hole in their back-play. For four hours before the game the rain came down and Cardiff Arms Park became greasy and treacherous. Teague, England's blind-side forward, had no time to discover even that.

Wales kicked off and Teague was one of the forwards waiting to anchor the ball. Wales came in behind the kick, there was a collision of bodies and bones and Teague was out cold – and out of the game. Gary Rees came off the bench and into the fray.

England still managed to chisel out a half-time lead of 9–6 but the rain intensified during the second half and so did the Welsh pressure, which largely came from two players – Norster at lock and Robert Jones at scrum-half. Norster kept winning the line-outs and Jones kept kicking the ball with great accuracy.

Within seconds of the start of the second half a high kick from Paul Turner, the Welsh fly-half, was gathered by Underwood but he missed Webb with his pass back. In swept Arthur Emyr, the Welsh wing, to hack the ball and Mike Hall, the centre, followed up and was awarded a try. Television replays suggested the referee, Kerry Fitzgerald of Australia, was incorrect, and that an English player had made the touch-down – but the score was in the book.

Wales still had to hold on to a 12–9 lead to win, but there was never much doubt that they would as England wasted their limited opportunities through poor distribution and the Welsh pack built up a head of steam which did not diminish. There were extraordinary scenes at the end with Thorburn making expansive gestures to the stands and, much later, describing one Welsh journalist as the "scum of the earth" at the official dinner. Thorburn was fired up beyond reason and the events of the day had clearly affected him greatly. He learned from the experience.

So England shared second place in the championship with Scotland. The two countries were allocated the largest number of players in the Lions' party, ten to England, nine to Scotland, with Calder as captain. Teague, who could remember hearing the national anthem at Cardiff and then nothing else, was a Lion. So was Ackford, after just five caps. So was Gareth Chilcott, the Bath prop, who had won 13 caps in five seasons, and so was Robinson.

Wales, who had become used to supplying many Lions over the years, this time had seven. Norster and Jones were naturally among them. As was Ieuan Evans, the Llanelli wing. "This is a chance which comes to so few," said Calder. "You have to give it your best shot."

When Carling withdrew from the party it clearly cost him a valuable chance to progress. McGeechan, a centre himself, was just the man to present Carling with more options, and a fully fit Carling, playing on hard grounds and without the responsibility of captaincy, would have been expected to shine. Now he was out.

The Lions called in Jeremy Guscott of Bath to replace him. He had not long completed the Pilkington Cup final in which Bath beat Leicester 10–6 and the invitations came flooding in. England wanted him to play against Romania at the 23 August stadium in Bucharest and the Lions wanted him for their 12-match tour.

Guscott's aim during the season had been to win a place in the South West team, which he achieved. He was also selected for England "B". By the time of the Cup final he was already in his 17th season with Bath having joined them as a seven-year-old in the mini-rugby section.

Guscott thus made history as the first player from the mini-rugby ranks to graduate to the England side. He had been missed or overlooked earlier at schools and colts level, where he rose no higher than the Somerset side; but Bath could see his potential, and after he had made two Cup final appearances for them as a replacement in 1985 and again in 1987 he began his push for the top. By the 1989 final Guscott

199

had played 113 times for the Bath first team and scored 66 tries. Some of those tries, breathtaking examples of perception, speed and finishing, were shown on television and everyone knew it was only matter of time before Guscott would be capped.

When England and the Lions called him up Guscott was two months short of his 24th birthday, which he celebrated the day before his spectacular Lions Test debut in Brisbane, and at 6ft 1in. and 13st. 3lb. was well built for the task. Fewer people realized then that Guscott had such a broad vision for the game, an awareness of the space and people around him, the options which might be available and the ability to react to them with lightning speed. Guscott does not like the idea of wearing No. 13 on his shirt and, it seems, never has. He should have taken that shirt on his debut in Romania, because that was Carling's number, but swapped with his Bath colleague Halliday.

England were the last of the home countries to go to Romania at senior level. "We are a little bit anxious because we don't know a lot about the opposition," said Geoff Cooke when the squad changed flights at Zurich's Kloten airport *en route* to Bucharest. "We will concentrate on the things which we do well."

There were two other new caps in the England side, Simon Hodgkinson, the Nottingham full back, and Steve Bates, the Wasps scrum-half. Hodgkinson was chosen because Webb was unavailable to travel; he was more than grateful for the opportunity. He had been in and out of the England squad for some time but early in the Cooke regime had played badly in the trial at Twickenham and had begun to wonder if his chance had gone.

England took two teams to Bucharest, the senior side and an under-21 side. Apart from all the equipment and supplies which normally accompany the players for away games, England also took hampers of food and drink because no one was certain what conditions would be like in Bucharest. The planning was fully justified.

200

England were well received and looked after, but they were told at the British Embassy not to take everything at face value and remember that the situation of the people in Bucharest might be worse than it seemed. The journalists who were in Bucharest with the squad found themselves carefully monitored but not oppressively so. You just had to assume that any Romanian who spoke to you had had security clearance because under the regime then, no contact with foreigners was permitted.

There was not a great deal of positive contact on the rugby field either. The under-21 team won the warm up match 54–13, with Neil Back, a flanker from the Midlands, scoring a hat trick of tries, and when England followed them out it was almost an identical story.

Led by Andrew, who had become his country's most capped fly-half during the championship, and with Carling watching in the stands, England marked their first appearance in Bucharest with a 58–3 win. The points began pouring in from the 14th minute, and among those who benefited were Guscott, who scored a hat trick, and Oti, who went one better with four tries. Hodgkinson converted all but one of the nine tries and also kicked a penalty.

Romania, who had beaten Wales in Cardiff the previous December, fielded 14 of the players who had started against the Welsh, but their heads dropped quickly and they were hopelessly inadequate for the task.

That night the Romanian Rugby Federation staged a fine banquet for the teams. There was much singing, demonstrations of folk dancing, and camaraderie – the spirit of rugby at work. However, there was not much sparkle in the dimly lit streets of Bucharest, just the ever-present security forces coldly eyeing a near-deserted city. Nine months later, Romania exploded into revolution and ended the regime and life of President Ceaucescu.

The walls and windows of the hotel where Romania and England had briefly linked in rugby unity were severely damaged in the street fighting which accompanied the revolution. The rugby club out in the suburbs, where England had trained, was part of an army complex and six Romanian rugby players would die defending it. The bullet holes in the walls and windows were still visible twelve months later

Almost one year on from England's visit, half of the England team were on duty for the four home Unions against the Rest of Europe in a match to raise funds to help Romanian rugby.

CHAPTER 30

The 1989 tour was vital to the future of the Lions. It was their first trip for eight years and there was little carry-over from 1983 except for two of the forwards, Robert Norster and Donal Lenihan. However, if the team may have lacked tour experience, coaches McGeechan and Uttley were fully aware of the Lions tradition and so was the manager of the tour to Australia, the former Welsh captain, Clive Rowlands.

Lions tours always fight against continuity because "the Lions" only exist within the context of the tour: they are born, then play and finally die with the last match. The Lions have only toured to the Southern Hemisphere - and played just a handful of special matches at home. The arrival of the World Cup, with its fresh demands on national teams and the search for improvement which followed, was a threat to the Lions; but the 1989 tourists met that head-on and passed on a challenge to their successors who will go to New Zealand in 1993.

It has often been said that Australian rugby does not merit a full Lions tour in its own right. Nobody could argue that Australia presented as severe a test as New Zealand or South Africa, where rugby is a national religion, but this did not mean that the Australians sat there, waiting for the Lions to stroll over them. "It's gonna be a jungle out there", said one poster advertising a Lions match in Brisbane. The poster was surprisingly accurate in its prediction.

The tour was unusual in that the Lions played six warm-up matches, including games against the premier states of Queensland and New South Wales, then hurled themselves into a frantic sequence of three Tests on successive Saturdays which was something no Lions team had ever been asked to do before.

The Lions duly won the six opening games, but not without loss. Paul Dean, the Irish fly-half, was injured after 25 minutes of the first game against Western Australia and had to return home. So did Chris Oti, who was hurt in his third game, against New South Wales, and did not play again.

The New South Wales match should have been played at Concord Oval but that was under water, which the England players were glad to hear, so the game was switched to the beautifully appointed North Sydney Oval where some of the stands have been brought from the Sydney Cricket Ground and carefully reinstated. It was on this pitch that the Lions were 20–21 down with a minute left before Chalmers rescued them with a dropped goal.

This put Chalmers into pole position for the fly-half role in the first Test, success in which was regarded as critical. The Lions chose a side which represented all four countries who had provided players, namely: Gavin Hastings (Scotland); Ieuan Evans (Wales), Mike Hall (Wales), Brendan Mullin (Ireland), Rory Underwood (England); Craig Chalmers (Scotland), Robert Jones (Wales); David Sole (Scotland), Brian Moore (England), David Young (Wales), Bob Norster (Wales), Paul Ackford (England), Derek White (Scotland), Finlay Calder (Scotland, capt.) and Dean Richards (England).

The first Test attracted 39,433 spectators to the Sydney Football Stadium and most of them must have believed that the Lions would win. They had been on the road long enough to have their drills worked out, Australia were likely to suffer from inactivity and the odds therefore favoured the tourists.

Instead Australia rose magnificently to the challenge and with an inspired performance won 30–12. They beat the Lions in the line-out, where they had expected to have difficulties, they were sharper in the loose play and Michael Lynagh had a masterly game at fly-half. Australia scored three tries, their opponents none.

The Lions were shattered. They knew how much hung on the opening Test and desperately wanted to take the initiative. Perhaps there was too much anxiety around for a side which had to face the reality that it had come together only a few weeks earlier.

Calder spoke for them all. "I don't believe for a minute that that was a true reflection of what we can do," he said. "We are all better people for that today and come next Saturday I would hope for better things. I am totally confident we can come back."

Anything positive that could be taken from the Test was picked up by the Lions on the Sunday morning and taken on to the next game against Australian Capital Territory at Canberra. This was not meant to be a difficult match for the Lions but when they were 8–21 behind approaching half-time, it had all the makings of a disaster, and the morale of the tour hung in the balance.

Fortunately the morale was in good hands because the midweek team, often led by Lenihan and consequently known as "Donal's Donuts" turned the game around to win 41–25 and in doing so stiffened the resolve within the squad as never before.

For the second Test they made the hugely significant change of leaving out Norster. Since he made his debut for Wales in 1982 he had become one of the best line-out forwards in the world and had won a record number of 34 caps. However, the Lions decided that his time was over and replaced him with Dooley, the man who had for so long regarded Norster as one of the three line-out forwards he truly respected (the other two are Ackford and Gary Whetton, the New Zealand captain).

So Dooley came into the Lions pack. As did Teague, in place of White. Scott Hastings and Guscott were chosen at centre and Andrew was promoted to fly-half. Andrew had been intending to spend his summer off from rugby by playing some cricket for Gerards Cross in the Thames Valley league, but here he was after three games pitched into the side which had to win to save the series.

There were all kinds of tensions around this Test at Brisbane. A brisk fight within the first few minutes between the two scrum-halves, Jones and Nick Farr-Jones, provided the first evidence of the intensity, and towards half-time a line-out disintegrated into a fight which involved some stamping by Young who was fortunate to escape a sending-off.

Overall, the Lions' pack hit a much higher level of play and their unity was compelling. Australia could not live with this new-found self-belief, and the Lions came hurtling through in the final 15 minutes to win 19–12 – and set up the tour for a winner-take-all finale the following week.

Guscott's Test debut was marked by the last try of the game. Heading for the Australian line he sensed that the Australian centres might close on him and shut the move down. So he chipped, low and hard, towards the posts and shouted at the ball, "Sit up, sit up." It did, straight into his hands, and the try was scored.

The Lions bubbled with confidence. McGeechan was delighted that they had at last discovered how to beat Australia in Australia, while Uttley now believed the forwards, with their driving play, in which Teague and Richards had played such major parts, had at times reached an exceptional level of control.

It was back to Sydney for the showdown. The atmosphere was such that everyone felt a tightening of the nerves through the week long build-up. Great choruses of "Waltzing Matilda" filled the air as the Australian fans prepared the scene for battle. The Lions had perhaps 500 hard-core supporters who had followed them through the series – and they made as much noise as they could.

Australia were 12–9 ahead early in the second half when a blatant error by Campese gave the Lions their only try. Campese had collected the ball after Andrew was wide with a dropped goal but threw a poor pass to his full back – and as the ball went loose Evans pounced through to score.

Gavin Hastings kicked two penalties after that to bring his tally to five and the Lions lead to 19–12. The match built to a nail-biting climax as Australia came back to trail by one point. Even the announcer had to enter the arena at that stage. "C'mon everyone," he said, "let's get behind this Australian side." But 19–18 it remained.

A long night followed. The Lions supporters filled the foyer of the hotel where the Test dinner was held and applauded the players, one by one, as they rode the escalator. The Lions thought it was one of the most moving moments of the tour and it made them realize what they had achieved and how hard it had been.

The Lions had not won a series since South Africa in 1974 when Willie John McBride was captain. McBride had toured with McGeechan and Uttley and would have been proud of their work. McGeechan was for ever reminding the players that when they played at home they went home to their families afterwards. On tour they had to go back to the other 29 players, and this had been one motivating factor all the way through.

The English players in the Test series were as proud as all the others. Teague was voted the man of the series but knew that the award was for everyone. Ackford had come from nowhere in less than a year to become the Lions front jumper. Dooley's abilities were recognized when he was brought in over Norster. The contribution of Richards was immense. This was the third Australian tour for Brian Moore, but the first that he had won. He could not wait for the new season to begin at home.

The English players could see what a force they were

becoming. Uttley was eager, too, to see what England could achieve. McGeechan was equally keen to see what his Scots could do on the back of their powerful contribution to the tour. What had happened with the Lions on the grounds of Australia was to lead to a unique match between Scotland and England eight months ahead.

CHAPTER 31

Richard Hill suffered a lengthy penalty for being captain of England in the 1987 match against Wales after which he, and three others, were suspended for one game. It is true he came back immediately into the World Cup squad, but thereafter Hill resumed duties behind the Bath pack and appeared to be out of favour. He did not help his cause one iota by being sent off in a club match in the autumn of 1988; but one year later he was brought back to the England squad and whatever kind of exile he had had to endure was over.

Hill was anxious to stake his claim to the England shirt once more. His involvement had begun more than five years before and if dedication to training and to playing were the only factors in winning caps he would probably have had more than anyone else. Only Hill knows the number of hours he has put in running the roads around his home and how many practice passes and kicks he has put in over the years, trying to make everything just that fraction better; all that, of course, on top of his training with Bath.

Carling was equally anxious to play again. His summer off had ended with a satisfactory report on his shin problem and he came through a seven-a-side tournament on a rock-hard pitch at Monte Carlo without any further difficulties.

However, while those two players were looking eagerly ahead, suddenly England suffered a considerable blow. Dean

Richards, back with his club at Leicester where he was captain for the first time, injured a shoulder in the first month of the season and was told he had to have an operation. In fact he had two operations – one to tighten his shoulder, a second to release a trapped nerve.

All this meant that Richards missed a complete season. He is not a very good spectator and rarely went to watch matches during his enforced lay-off. Not until the summer of 1990 did he test his shoulder in a "contact situation" when he came on for half a game for the British Police during a tour of Romania. The heat was intense and he felt the pace badly – but his shoulder was fine.

Richards is one of those players who simply does not set himself targets. He has always played rugby to enjoy himself and regards everything else which has come his way as a bonus. This is perhaps why he was able to detach himself from the game that he could not play and why, when England played Scotland in the Grand Slam decider in 1990, he was on duty at a Leicester City soccer match at Filbert Street – albeit with one ear on the radio commentary.

Fiji were autumn opponents in 1989 for both Scotland and England. The Scots took them on first and won 38–17. There was a particularly impressive performance from Tony Stanger, the Harwick wing, who scored two tries in his first game for his country.

This score threw down the gauntlet for England to do even better. Deliberately England had not chosen what might be regarded as their best side because they gave first caps to two props, Mark Linnett, a policeman from Moseley, and Andy Mullins of Harlequins. Hodgkinson and Guscott both had their first matches for England at Twickenham.

Fiji often play some of the most beautiful rugby to be seen on the world stage but they were in a bitter mood this day and guilty of some appalling behaviour. The referee Brian Stirling handed out numerous warnings and sent off two of the Fijian backs when those warnings were not heeded.

In the midst of all the mayhem England produced some

powerful football to win 58–23. Underwood's five tries equalled a record set in 1907 and brought his total try count for England to 18, which also equalled a record. The England forwards played well, Hill and Andrew hit a solid understanding at half back and the England backs looked good with the ball in their hands. It was an ideal start to the winter.

New Zealand, meanwhile, were savouring conditions in Britain and Ireland two years ahead of their defence of the World Cup. They beat Wales 34–9 and Ireland 23–6, then progressed to a sign-off game against the Barbarians at Twickenham which they won 21–10.

The England management took a close look at the All Blacks and decided that the England team of the time would not have beaten them. They thought that New Zealand were faster and fitter and overall knew precisely what they wanted to do in any part of the pitch. They also thought that the New Zealand front row was exceptional, and that while Richard Loe and Steve McDowell were at prop they would cause problems for anybody. All this, of course, was two years ahead of England playing New Zealand in World Cup II...

England put in another warm-weather training camp prior to the 1990 championship, using the Club La Santa facilities on the Canary island of Lanzarote. Here Carling expressed the view that England were progressing on the right lines and that the difference between good and great required a little sacrifice, a little effort, and then things might happen.

Cooke promised the squad an 18-month programme culminating in the World Cup which would be the most intensive they had faced. Each player would know what was required of him, with training patterns laid out and monitored. Aspects of mental preparation aimed at improving concentration and positive thinking were heavily underlined. Everything had to be locked into place and understood.

Back from Lanzarote and its balmy atmosphere, England were plunged into a swirling wind at Twickenham against Ireland and had to battle for more than one hour before unleashing their backs and ending the game on a high note. Two tries through the forwards, one by Probyn and a second by David Egerton who was at No. 8, set England on the way. However, it was a flick pass from Guscott which sent Underwood speeding for the corner and a record-breaking try, and then a stunning run from Carling which put Guscott through and gave the match such a compelling finish. It was 23–0 to England – and a confident squad prepared to go to France.

Next door to the Parc des Princes in Paris is the Stade Jean Bouin and most of the time there are two airhalls on site, providing indoor tennis facilities. They were standing there on the morning of 3 February 1990, but they had gone by lunchtime because the winds thundering in from the east tore them from their mountings. It was in these testing conditions that the England "B" team drew 15–15 with France shortly before the championship match, and those conditions persisted inside the oval bowl of the main stadium. Advertising hoardings fell like playing cards, rubbish was whipped up and blown from the pitch surround into the seats.

That was what faced France and England, but it made not the slightest difference to Hodgkinson. His first three penalties had to be struck low and hard; he put two of them straight between the posts, and although he hit an upright with the other England were on their way.

Then Andrew, heading left away from a line-out, suddenly braked and switched direction to kick deep to the France line. Underwood hurtled after the ball and touched down for a try, and with Hodgkinson kicking a third penalty England were ahead 13–0 at half-time. Uttley had been saying the previous day that England enjoyed being in Paris because it brought them even closer together as a squad; but now the thousands of England supporters who were in the ground began to make their presence felt as well.

Straight after half-time, Carling charged down a kick and Guscott managed to put his boot to the ball and regain it from the bounce to run on and score. At the end Carling, with immaculate finishing, broke outside Serge Blanco and finished the game off at 26–7.

A similar scoring pattern emerged against Wales at Twickenham. Hodgkinson kicked two penalties in ten minutes before Carling smashed his way through a suspect Welsh defence to score in the corner. The England forwards knew from an early stage that the Welsh pack seemed short on fitness and combat readiness, and apart from the gritty defiance of Phil Davies this assumption held good.

Underwood scored two more tries in this game, one after an interception which left him with 75 yards to run, and the 34–6 win was topped off with a try by Hill and more goals from Hodgkinson. The England crowd had so rarely been treated to anything like this against Wales, as the record score indicated, and loved it all – especially when some of their favourite forwards, particularly Moore, showed they wanted to run just as much as the backs.

So England were three wins up with Scotland to play for the Grand Slam. The euphoria afterwards was immense. Uttley described it as "the most outstanding performance that any of us have witnessed from any England side. There was a stamp of greatness about this side."

Over the weekend the Welsh coach, John Ryan, resigned to be succeeded by Ron Waldron, the Neath coach. The Welsh politely said they thought England would beat Scotland and went on with trying to solve their own problems. Everyone was saying that England would beat Scotland – everyone, that is, except the Scots.

David Sole, who had succeeded Finlay Calder as Scottish captain, had been following in England's footsteps in terms of the sequence of matches and while England had one month to wait before playing Scotland the Scots still had to face Wales.

Scotland won 13–9 and the mega-match was set up: Scotland v. England on 17 March 1990, which would be for the most rewarding package available in the championship – the

213

Grand Slam, the Calcutta Cup, the Five Nations' title and the Triple Crown.

South of the border few were saying that England would lose. Here was an ambitious and expansive England team which had scored three tries against Ireland, three against France and four against Wales.

"If the players sat down and thought of all the implications they would be pretty nervous," said Carling a couple of days before the game. "But there is a calmness about this side, no great tension, and we know exactly what we have to do. The Scots have a rough idea of how we will play but it will be wiser for both sides to use the latest information rather than hark back to what happened on the Lions tour last summer."

The Scots were saying very little. There were no promises or threats and a low-key approach took their side quietly towards a match which had gripped Edinburgh and all points Scottish around the world as never before.

On the Friday Edinburgh began to bulge with supporters from both camps. As the city settled for the night the wind began to increase but England, asleep in their hotel in Peebles were unaware.

The wind had strengthened by the morning and McGeechan and some of the Scottish players went to the ground early to have a look around and check how kicking might be affected. It was a small but significant point – because Scotland played with the wind when the match began.

Before the game started, there were two other highly emotive factors in Scotland's favour. One was the decision to walk on to the pitch instead of run. Each step by the Scottish players was a definite statement of whose territory this was and how much they intended to keep it. The second was the singing of "Flower of Scotland", each word hanging on the air, drifting into the minds of the players it was intended to lift.

So the stage was set and the initiative was immediately taken by Scotland with two successful penalties, downwind, in the first ten minutes. This was the first time that England

214

had been behind in the championship that season and the first time they had been behind in any match for an entire year.

What England needed was a score to settle them and it came very quickly with a break by Teague, Hill and Carling which left Guscott to dummy his way through for a try. Next England set up camp on the Scotland line but the resistance was massive, and although the England forwards clearly thought they could drive over and break the Scottish will, nothing happened. They opted for scrums when they might have let Hodgkinson kick at goal and for a while there was a lack of clarity about the tactical requirements. It was grimly reminiscent of a match in Dublin in 1970 when Wales, then favourites, argued amongst themselves about who should be doing what and lost 14–0.

A third penalty from Chalmers gave Scotland the lead 9–4 at half-time. Scotland's interventionist tactics were working superbly, England were not creating the control they had anticipated in the line-out, the Scottish back row was operating magnificently, slicing into the England framework so that one area of the team became separated from the next and a blue shirt often stood where a white one ought to have been. Out in the middle of the pitch there was no longer any way through for Carling or Guscott.

The critical score was immediately after half-time. England took a scrum on half-way but Teague knocked on as he tried to pick up. The scrum was given to Scotland, there was a thrust by Jeffrey, another thrust by Armstrong, then Gavin Hastings was into space and kicked ahead. The ball stood up high for the advancing Stanger who took possession and scored.

That was 13–4 to Scotland, and although Hodgkinson narrowed the margin with a penalty 13 minutes later, the Scots stuck firm. England's pressure never flagged but the day ended with the blues taking victory, 13–7.

At the end the two teams could barely come to terms with what had happened. Scotland's players were caught like clothes in a tumble drier as they tried to cut a path through the massed crowds back to the dressing room. All England's men wanted to do was run and hide. "I now know the true meaning of the word 'gutted'," said Uttley a full two days later.

Edinburgh was a split city that evening, most celebrating, some commiserating. There were plenty of people ready to stick they knife into Carling's captaincy, or lack of it as they perceived it, but within the camp nobody was apportioning blame. They knew that Scotland had foiled them, that a team which put together all the classic ingredients which make up an underdog had cut down the favourites. England's players looked dazed but it was in the hours after Murrayfield that a new determination was created.

Out of all the words that have been spoken and written about that day one phrase has stuck in my mind. It was said to me sometime after midnight by John Burgess, the chairman of England's World Cup committee, as we walked along Princes Street. "It is the end of the beginning," he said. The more events unfolded the more he was proved right.

On the Sunday morning Carling was out of Edinburgh on one of the early flights south because that afternoon he provided comment on a women's rugby match at Moseley for a television programme. On the Monday night Carling was a guest – with McGeechan and Jeffrey – on a BBC television show hosted by Terry Wogan. Carling wore one of his favourite shirts, striped purple and white, and one of the things he said was an epitaph to the campaign. "We are desperately upset," he said, "but we have had great fun and a lot of people have enjoyed watching us play."

Bill and Pam Carling, who had lived through a whole gamut of emotions from the time they had lunch before the game with the parents of David Sole, the Scotland captain, to long, long afterwards, returned home to discover that they had been burgled. Among the items taken was a video recorder, timed and set to record the Scotland–England match. They did not seek a replacement.

CHAPTER 32

When the initial impact of the Murrayfield defeat had subsided, England began to look for positive factors. "If we look back on the season as a whole I have been able to take some succour and a lot of pride from the style and manner in which we played the games before Scotland," said Uttley. "Against Scotland there were moments when we showed we have come a long way down the road establishing us as a major force."

The management resisted being judged on the one performance. The loss was categorized in much the same vein as the end of the 1989 championship at Cardiff – an England defeat against a highly motivated team in a hostile atmosphere and with a referee from a Southern Hemisphere country – Australia in 1989, New Zealand in 1990. There was a danger that England were becoming neurotic about Australian or New Zealand referees, but they had had some unsatisfactory results with these referees and Uttley was right to put the matter into perspective: "We have to get to a point where we can cope with all things," he stressed. "We are not good enough currently, and I am confident we can overcome these problems."

Uttley knew it was impossible to pick and choose when to win a Grand Slam but when England did so in 1991 it did cross his mind that he would rather take the Slam on the eve of the World Cup than one year earlier. It was not something he could forecast in 1990.

Cooke assessed the season: "Despite the intense disappointment of not winning the Grand Slam it has been successful. England scored more points in the championship than any other side in history and had record-breaking wins against France and Wales. The team played with pace, power and style and provided a great deal of enjoyment for spectators and also provided a worthwhile role model for club players and thousands of youngsters. I still believe we are on course to make a serious challenge in the World Cup in 1991 but I think it will be extremely important to us to win the five nations' championship next year. The first match against Wales in Cardiff will be crucial in that respect."

England had one more match to play after the championship. This took them to Rovigo, a new venue for them, to play an Italian team. England retained just six of their regular side, sufficient to win by 33–15 on a sticky, dusty evening. One bonus was the return of Oti who had been out of rugby since the Lions tour the previous June. He scored a try and came off smiling, the blue shirt of his opposing wing draped over his bare shoulders.

Carling did not complete the match. With a quarter of an hour left he came off, looking dazed, and the effects of a gruelling season were written all over him. His ribs hurt and his face was bruised but he was able to walk off. A little later that year, also in Italy, it was possible to see the wear and tear on another England captain, Bryan Robson, in the soccer World Cup when he was also forced out by injury. In his career Robson had broken a leg three times, dislocated a shoulder on several occasions, broken a finger and a nose, and had a host of less severe injuries. Carling could never want to match that list.

The soccer World Cup pushed another England team further on to the sporting stage because they reached the semi-finals before being beaten by West Germany and Italy. The World Cup final brought Germany and Argentina into conflict in a poor advertisement for the world's most played and most watched team game, and by coincidence afterwards the Argentina soccer team and the England rugby team arrived in Buenos Aires within a matter of hours of each other.

Argentina scurried back after the World Cup final. England, on a much lower key, were opening up rugby contacts with Argentina for the first time since the Falklands conflict in 1982. Quite apart from the games they would play, the diplomatic significance of the trip was considerable because the presidents of the Rugby Unions of England, Scotland, Ireland and Wales were all there as well.

Unfortunately for England some of their best players were not. Of the backs who might have been considered Rory Underwood, Jeremy Guscott, Simon Halliday, Mark Bailey and Rob Andrew were not available. Paul Ackford and Gary Pearce, two of the more experienced forwards, were also unavailable.

England had to try a number of players who were still in the development stage. The tour flew in the face of the theory that these days you only take your best players – but if the mission worked England would have more positive information on their material.

There was also the political aspect. Quite clearly the England rugby team was construed in many parts of Argentina as visible proof that the relationship between the two countries was fully on the mend. The Rugby Union president, Michael Pearey, a retired Royal Navy officer, spoke as a serviceman and a rugby player, and always referred back to the Falklands before expressing the wish that all future conflicts would be on the sporting field and nowhere else.

England were the guests at the first formal party in the residence of the British Ambassador in Buenos Aires for eight years. The official Embassy comment was that the tour had made the work of the British delegation "immeasurably easier". Carling was described as the "No. 1 diplomat" by the Ambassador. The accompanying press party were invited to breakfast with the President of Argentina, Carlos Menem.

Against this background England still had to play some football. The tour was structured so that the team played in Buenos Aires in the same stadium on four successive Saturdays, with three other midweek games in provincial cities.

England lost three of their first four games. By the time they chose their first Test team, which included four new caps in Nigel Heslop, the Orrell wing, David Pears, the Harlequins fly-half, Jason Leonard, a prop from Saracens, and Dean Ryan, the Wasps' No. 8, there was an air of deep concern about where England were heading. In the countdown to the first international Carling kept stressing the need for pride, for the experienced players to adapt, for the younger ones to rise to the challenge.

The first Test went well, mirroring some of the matches in the previous year because Hodgkinson started them off with two penalties and a try went in, via Ryan, after 19 minutes. The platform was established and England went on to win 25–12.

One week later the same England team tried again and at 10–6 after half an hour, with tries on the board from Hodgkinson and Heslop, another victory looked certain. But Dooley, such a vital player in an untried team, had been struggling with a rib problem and early in the second half had to come off. England's drive went with him and slowly they were overhauled by Argentina's goal-kicker, Hernan Vidou, whose five penalties won the match 15–13.

Deep dismay surrounded the final hours of England's stay in Argentina. Everyone knew it was black spot on England's record because they had not lost to Argentina before. Their hosts had joined an exclusive club and the knowledge hurt. Cooke criticized the coaching system in England, reminding his small audience in the foyer of the Sheraton Hotel in Buenos Aires that "England are a product of what is happening in our clubs, counties, and divisions".

Cooke went on to say that the aim was not to beat Argentina

but to develop players. In that area the arrival of Leonard and Heslop was successful. Both were to remain in the side. While Argentina joined the ranks of all those who caused sporting upsets in 1990 (Buster Douglas, Chris Eubank, Mr Frisk, Crystal Palace and the Scotland rugby team were some of the others) England just wanted to go home and start again.

There was a final irony to come. The captain of their flight out of Buenos Aires welcomed them on board as the "very successful British soccer team".

CHAPTER 33

A terrible frustration was now beginning to gnaw away in the minds of showcase players of rugby world-wide. There had been agitation for some time for the game to loosen its regulations on amateurism and permit players to earn money from activities such as writing books, broadcasting and public speaking, television, films and personal appearances.

All administrative aspects of rugby on a world basis are under the control of the International Rugby Football Board of which the leading countries are members. The Board makes decisions and the Rugby Unions implement them – from changes in the laws governing the way the game is played to the timing and structure of tours.

The Board started to review the amateur regulations in 1989 and by the end of that year had agreed to changes. However, they would not allow players to earn money from playing the game or to benefit from advertising or promotional activities directly related to rugby.

The whole issue was so fundamental that by the spring of 1991 it still remained open to discussion – and in England's case still awaited agreement between the Rugby Union and the players about what was permitted. The subject has been on such shifting ground that any prediction here might easily be invalidated; but the two sides of the argument are worth stating.

Those who sought change said that the leading players had now entered a phase where they were having to devote so much more of their spare time to preparing for international matches, to making tours and to improving fitness that some form of compensation should be available. Those against change argued that rugby's very strength came from its belief in and maintenance of amateurism and that the demands on players' time, while increasing, had in fact been accompanied by changes in the framework of the game which required them to play fewer big matches.

The World Cup had altered thinking among the leading nations, and no one wanted to miss out on the money that could be made. England were already two-thirds of the way to a proper playing structure, and the success of the English game had brought more interest, revenue and sponsorship than ever before.

Some of the early forecasts on what the players might earn under the proposed framework were staggeringly off target. Sums involving thousands of pounds were predicted once players jumped on the new gravy train and began to be paid for their off-field activities. It was misleading and mis-chievous – and was bound to disturb players.

England began the winter of 1990 knowing that the issue was to be discussed by the International Board at a special meeting in Edinburgh in October, but anyone who expected hard and fast rulings was in for disappointment. It was agreed that players could earn money for their off-the-field activities, but each country had to decide what it would allow.

This led to even more frustration for the England players. They were regarded by players in the other home countries as pace-setters for the revised structure, but they made little progress throughout the season and were still discussing matters with the Rugby Union when it ended.

The majority of the England squad formed themselves into a company called "Player Vision" to conduct non-rugby-related business. A company called "WHJ Promotions", which was run by the former England cricket captain Bob

Willis and his brother David, entered into an agreement with Player Vision.

The England players were largely united and had come to certain decisions amongst themselves. They came from a team background so everything they planned had to be on a team basis. No player should be in a position to earn more on the back of the efforts of the others.

For a few weeks in the middle of the season Willis seemed to attract more attention than the players he was representing. At the same time the Rugby Union was carrying out discussions with a small group of senior players on what could be the way forward.

Nothing happened; but the eventual split between the players and WHJ Promotions was one reaction to the aftermath of the Wales–England match which began the 1991 championship. WHJ had sought an interview fee from the BBC on behalf of the players. That was turned down, and as a result none of the England management nor any of the players attended the customary post-match interviews.

Carling could not avoid being in at the sharp end of all this. He saw it as part of his responsibilities that he should identify with and lead the players in the cause. Time and again he stressed that no one wanted to be paid for playing the game, but he could not see any harm in players being able to earn from endorsements or advertising.

All the argument and debate in the corridors of power might have had an adverse effect on the way England prepared and played their matches, but the opposite was true. The more England were criticized for pursuing commercial targets, the more they drew together and the stronger they became.

The debate on payments to players had hardly gathered momentum when England began their playing commitments. Dean Richards was available once more after his year off and in the first month of the season returned for the match against the Barbarians, who were celebrating their centenary.

The Baa-baas, as is their custom, had drawn together a

224

side of runners and adventurers, digging into a high level of talent for their first match against England: the styles of New Zealand, France, Australia, Wales, Ireland and Scotland could all be found in their team.

England knew they were on a hiding to nothing. They were expected to win, as a national side playing scratch opponents. They also recognized that the Barbarians would not keep within the parameters normally associated with international football. However, after David Campese's try had put the Barbarians in front, the England side's long-established teamwork helped them to take control when it was necessary, and with a try by Richards and 14 points from Hodgkinson England held on to win 18–16. A different Barbarians side played against Wales a week later and won 31–24.

England did not award caps against the Barbarians but full caps were available for the match with Argentina at Twickenham. The only new selection was the hooker, John Olver. He had been at school some years before with Peter Winterbottom before going on to join Harlequins and captain them in the 1988 Cup final. Olver had also sat on the England bench on numerous occasions as understudy to Brian Moore and this time they reversed roles, so ending a run of 22 caps for Moore. Moore and Olver had changed clubs at the start of the season. Moore had come to London from Nottingham and joined Harlequins, Olver had gone to Northampton.

Another player in the front row who had changed clubs was Jason Leonard, a self-employed carpenter and joiner who came from Barking in Essex. He had left Saracens for Harlequins and now appeared to have ended the long run at loose-head prop of Paul Rendall, who had had 27 caps. Leonard did not realize how demanding the season would be for him. He had to drive considerable distances to train and play for Harlequins, and put in hours of extra work to improve his fitness. The rewards, however, were there: a Grand Slam with England and the Pilkington Cup with Harlequins.

225

There was one far-reaching selection change against Argentina. Jon Hall had not been in the England side since 1987, when he was forced to drop out of the World Cup squad with injury, but it was felt that his current form and proven ability at flanker earned him a place to the exclusion of Teague. Hall's line-out work and his pace had gained him the recall, but clearly it was one of the hardest decisions for the management to take – and one which was to be overturned by a further injury to Hall at the start of 1991.

Carling quickly cut out any speculation on the need for revenge against Argentina. His target was a number of good victories prior to the World Cup and this was to be one of them. He had his wish, because England so dominated Argentina that all the running skills and finishing associated with the championship earlier in the year came flowing back. England scored seven tries and Hodgkinson kicked almost every goal and the result was 51–0. Argentina were totally shattered, and long before the end their forwards had run out of steam. All of them, that is, except their 18-year-old prop Federico Mendez.

Mendez might have had a boy's age but he was physically impressive, weighing over 17st. and standing 6ft 1in. There was nothing unusual in that, but what was unusual was his right-hand punching power, which he demonstrated close to the end to the extreme discomfort of Ackford. Mendez came from behind to punch Ackford on the jaw – and laid him out. Exit Mendez and Ackford – one sent off, the other helped off. Mendez was suspended for four weeks and Argentina claimed he was provoked by Probyn, the England prop. The Rugby Union looked into the incident but took no further action.

Overall, England's autumn programme had gone well. There were two months to go before the training session in Lanzarote and everyone in the squad went back to their clubs and divisions hoping to be included on the trip to the Canaries.

Carling had been nursing an ankle injury and had not been

100 per cent fit against Argentina. It might have been time for him to stay out of the limelight for a while, but not a bit of it. Even though England had no further games their captain, for one reason or another, made news more often than he might have liked.

For a start, there were allegations about money. Someone wrote to the Rugby Union claiming that Carling had broken the amateur regulations as they stood 18 months earlier by accepting money at a non-rugby function. Yes, said the accused player, he had received money and that money had gone to charity.

Carling himself said he had turned down an offer of £400,000 to join a Rugby League club. The offer had been made by Warrington earlier in the year. He had to answer an accusation that he had taken money for appearing in non-rugby-related photographs in a magazine. Wherever Carling turned over a period of several weeks the link between him and money was being made; but a young man in such a prominent position had to accept that he would attract attention, especially when he began driving a top-of-the-range Mercedes.

Carling also created other problems for himself, perhaps unwittingly. For instance, when he strayed away from rugby during a question-and-answer session at the annual conference of the Central Council of Physical Recreation and criticized Paul Gascoigne for his behaviour in a soccer match, the press reaction was guaranteed.

Gascoigne was a cult figure at the time. Carling had watched the England mid-field player on television in a match between Tottenham and Liverpool and observed: "I have not seen so petulant a performance as that from Gascoigne in a long time. There was an obvious abuse of the referee. If that had happened in my sport there would have been a lot of soul-searching and possibly disciplinary action for the man involved. If Gascoigne is allowed to behave in such a manner, is it any wonder there is trouble on the terraces? The Football Association has a lot to answer for."

Carling's comments came up when he was being questioned on fair play in sport. The soccer world quickly retaliated, pointing out that players should not cross over from their own sport to another and criticize. Carling, of course, was being honest about what he felt; but it was yet another incident which was teaching him to say less, publicly, in the months which lay ahead. Privately, he apologized to Gascoigne. A few weeks after he had done so, Gascoigne was sent off – for swearing at a referee.

There was further trouble with London in the divisional championship. Carling not only failed to turn up for training (on his 25th birthday) but did not tell London that he would be absent. London's attitude to that was the same as it would have been to any player involved in the same scenario. Carling was dropped for one game.

Interspersed with these matters of fact were the rumours that Carling wanted to quit the England captaincy and also leave his club, Harlequins, for another. Cooke, as manager, quickly dismissed speculation on the captaincy by saying: "I don't know where all this talk about him has come from. I have spoken to him about it and told him I'm very happy with his performances for England. We always said he would learn and develop as a leader."

Harlequins acted quickly as well. Chairman Roger Looker commented in a club programme: "A growing band of scribes seem to be suggesting that Harlequin Football Club is unhappy with the approach of the England captain. I admit to confusion as I have certainly not been asked my opinion and neither has the Honorary Secretary, nor any member of the Playing Committee.

I want to make it clear that we have all been very impressed with Will's commitment this season. Indeed he should probably have come off earlier in the Liverpool–St Helen's game. He cannot score three times from our own 22 in every game he plays. Neither do we expect or want him to play if he is not fit.

"Will is a very important member of the first XV squad

and because of his strength and skill he attracts the attention of the opposition to the degree that it often gives others more room in which to beat the opposition than would normally occur.

"He has the demanding role both on and off the field of England captain and in our opinion he has worked very hard to publicize and popularize the game in this country. We are proud to have the England captain in the club and I know Will is proud to be a Harlequin."

Such confidence in him and clear speaking helped clear the air. Will Carling ended 1990 as he began it – as England captain, as a member of Harlequins and as an amateur.

CHAPTER 34

Historically, 1991 will take some beating. Whatever else happened the final of the World Cup was to be held in England's home at Twickenham and there was no escaping the countdown to the greatest sporting event in England since the 1966 soccer World Cup. Players prayed for form and fitness to hold, administrators checked and double-checked their planning, agents and sponsors did their sums, referees prayed for error-free matches – and everyone wondered how to obtain a ticket. As for the England squad, 1991 came in marked by a three-hour delay at London's Gatwick airport as they waited to fly to Lanzarote.

By the time England had landed at Arrecife airport and taken a coach journey to the other side of the island, one of their planned training sessions had already had to be abandoned. Otherwise almost everything clicked into shape on the four-day training trip which was aimed specifically at beating Wales in Cardiff two weeks later.

Club La Santa, England's base for a second year, has a grass pitch, a training track and an indoor training area among its facilities. Everything is within walking distance of the apartments which the players shared, two to a room: it was an ideal place for England to draw together.

Cooke, Uttley and Elliott had developed the England squad so that it had a club atmosphere. Of course players came and went for all kinds of reasons but the hard core remained, carefully monitored. Lanzarote offered the management the chance to remind the squad of their objectives and obligations in World Cup year.

The players who were chosen to go to Lanzarote knew that they were the élite of the day, with so much beckoning on the horizon. At the same time, the team to play Wales had not been announced. This meant there was competition for places, which manifested itself in some of the most rigorous and combative training which any England squad has ever produced. It was in one of these sessions that Hall, only two months on from his return to the side, hurt a knee and ruled himself out of the Welsh game. Moore, desperate for reinstatement as the No. 1 hooker, pinched a nerve and remained doubtful for some days. These injuries made Cooke decide not to announce a team while the squad was in Lanzarote, as had been planned.

It was ironic that Hall should be injured because in the fitness sessions his rival for the No. 6 shirt, Teague, had produced some outstanding performances which made those who analyze the figures draw breath. They knew that Teague must have been working spectacularly hard to achieve such levels.

All the other testing produced satisfactory results. The players knew that there was no escape from the testing and that they could have no excuses. On that basis England were ready for the championship. As Cooke observed: "The general impression is that we are pretty much on course. It is all a progressive build-up, and from our point of view we are coming up to the first peak."

In Wales the previous month the opinion was expressed that England were wasting their time going to train in warm and dry conditions in Lanzarote for a match in Cardiff where it was likely to be cold and wet. In particular, Ron Waldron, the Welsh coach, thought it was better to meet as a squad at home.

This missed the point. England did not go to Lanzarote

looking for a copy of conditions in Cardiff. They went to Lanzarote to perfect, in excellent weather, all the drills which they wanted to use against Wales. Almost everything they did to produce their first win at Cardiff in 28 years was talked about, worked on and worked on again, in the Canaries.

The togetherness of being in Lanzarote was another important factor. England's players are split over wide areas of the country in terms of their homes and clubs, and contact outside of training is minimal. The hours in training camp were vital for bonding players, especially on the eve of the championship.

It was also noticeable that squad members were beginning to draw into themselves and put up barriers. Nobody, from Carling onwards, was making any promises about the championship in general or the Welsh game in particular. "Every game I play is important to me. Wales will be a hard international away game," was about all Carling wanted to say.

A week after returning from Lanzarote Cooke confirmed the side. There were no surprises. Teague was in the back row, Moore was at hooker, and the 15 men who were to begin at Cardiff were to play unaltered through the championship, the first time that had happened for 31 years.

Cooke's first visit to Cardiff had been in 1989, and what he saw and heard that day led to changes of plan for the 1991 match. "I found it a quite unpleasant experience," he says. "I was quite taken aback by the obvious depth of hatred which is generated there, which manifested itself on the day of the England–Wales game. People had told me about it but it still struck me. It was like going into a war zone."

For 1991 Cooke and the management team decided that England would stay in the heart of Cardiff instead of some miles away. They even chose a hotel which overlooked Cardiff Arms Park. They trained in Cardiff and they mixed with the people and they heard what the people were saying. The Welsh anthem, which is said to have made so many opponents tremble, was constantly played to the England team so that it would hold no terrors for them on the day.

232

In the two years since England had been at Cardiff Wales had lost so many players through injury and defections to Rugby League that only three, Thorburn, Ieuan Evans and Robert Jones, bridged the gap. Eight England players remained from 1989. It may just have been a factor.

England walked to the stadium from their hotel, knowing that the previous evening seven hours of rain had fallen. However, they kicked off with the sun behind them and almost immediately went 0–3 behind to a penalty by Thorburn.

This was not in England's planning at all, but very quickly they started to establish their presence up-front. Wales conceded penalties as they tried to halt the pressure, and Hodgkinson exacted full retribution, kicking four goals in the first half for England to lead 12–3.

Wales were expected to buckle against the England pack, but did nothing of the sort, and when early in the second half Neil Jenkins, their 19-year-old fly-half, took over the kicking after Thorburn had missed four times he earned huge cheers for reducing the margin to 12–6.

Yet the formula had been set. England's forwards pincered Wales in most areas of activity and Hodgkinson kicked three more penalties to bring his total to seven – a world record. Teague, injured within seconds two years earlier and clearly a marginal selection this time, scored the only try of the game, driving in from Richards's pick-up.

England's victory had been clinically achieved. No risks had been taken, no mistakes made with which Wales could turn the game. Even though the players claimed that all that backlog of defeat at Cardiff was nothing to do with them and was not their fault, they knew deep down that they had rolled away one of the great rocks which had sat on English rugby. Around 120 players had worn the England shirt at Cardiff since 1963 and had gone home beaten. It was time for a change, even if it was an anti-climax because of the uneventful way in which England had performed.

The usual activity followed the game. In the Cardiff press

233

area in the North stand words were flowing to newspapers. In the broadcasting area in the South stand the live commentaries were over and the next phase, interviews with players and coaches, was about to begin. It was shortly afterwards that the word came back to the press room that England were not going to attend any interviews unless they were paid £5,000. That story was checked with Jonathan Price, marketing manager of the Welsh Rugby Union, and found to be incorrect.

It was then learned that England were not going to send any representatives to the press conference which the Welsh Rugby Union hold in the gymnasium under the South stand. That too was checked and was found to be true. Suddenly the ending of 28 years of history sank into the background in the light of these developments. What were England up to?

Anyone who has observed journalists in action will know that the collective agony of a press corps deprived of what it perceives to be its rights has to be seen to be believed – and a whole pack of us set off for the Crest Hotel, in which the England squad was resident. One aspect of journalism is called "door-stepping". This is a phrase which roughly describes hanging around anywhere where a news situation might be developing. In some cases the pace can be forced – and after about an hour of waiting in the foyer of the Crest Hotel it was decided to do just that.

Small groups of journalists roamed the hotel looking for the England management and players. Cooke was in his room and, annoyed at being disturbed, threatened to call the hotel security staff. Some of the security staff wanted to remove the intruders but a senior member of the hotel management defused that, recognizing that genuine journalists were trying to do a genuine job.

Everyone knew that the players would not stay in their rooms for ever – they had a commitment to attend the Welsh Rugby Union dinner for the teams at the Angel Hotel across the street. A few players came through the foyer of the hotel but most of them used a back route avoiding contact. Don Rutherford, the technical director of the Rugby Union, made the only official comment at this stage of the evening, saying the decision not to speak had been taken by the players before the game and that now they wanted to reflect on their next match.

In my own movements around the Crest Hotel I entered a lift and there found Carling and another person, a stranger to both of us. I said why I was there and told Carling that the situation of the England captain and management not giving interviews was so unusual that I felt an explanation was necessary. There was still an accusation that a cash row was at the heart of it all. Carling replied: "I'm sorry, I can't help you, I can't comment." The stranger, who had heard the discussion, then said to Carling: "Don't take any notice of the ***** press. Tell them to **** off. After what you have done today for English rugby, you can tell them all to **** off." Carling did not act on that advice.

About half an hour after this, the scene moved to the Angel Hotel where Denis Evans, the secretary of the Welsh Rugby Union, was appraised of what was happening and asked if he would request Dudley Wood, the secretary of the Rugby Union, to speak to the press. Evans did so but said that Wood would not come out of the dinner because "it was a matter for the players".

However, Wood did emerge and so did Captain Michael Pearey, the president of the Rugby Union. Pearey said immediately that he was going to make a public apology at the dinner for the discourtesy of the England players and management in not seeing the press. Pearey strongly denied that money was involved in the decision by the players and said that they had felt that after this game, of all games, they would be likely to be drained and wanted time to reflect before they spoke to anyone. Pearey admitted he thought that the action was ill-advised and that the pressure of coming to Wales had "got through to the players".

Wood hoped that it was a one-off situation and said it was

unsatisfactory. As secretary of the game's governing body he felt he should have been warned about what was developing. "It would have been helpful," he said.

Press conferences are a fact of life in most major sports. They have been part of rugby union for some years now – certainly well before Cooke, Elliott and Uttley formed the England management – and have become accepted on both sides as a method of acquiring and disseminating information.

Sometimes what is said at press conferences following England matches is barely reported at all. Now there was a case of a non-conference giving England more headlines than even their historic win over Wales had created. Of course it sowed a seed of doubt that their public relations would ever be the same again.

CHAPTER 35

Apologies came thick and fast. Cooke, to whom good public relations seemed second nature, accepted responsibility and was subsequently reprimanded by the Rugby Union. Carling also apologized. "We just wanted 24 hours to come to terms with a match that represented something so special to the players," he said. If Cooke and Carling were guilty of anything it was underestimating the effects of their actions.

My understanding of the events is that representatives of the players did indeed ask BBC television for £5,000 for interviews (of recorded, as opposed to live material), but when this request was presented to the Rugby Union the answer was that the players were not entitled to such a payment under the prevailing regulations. The issue of the press conference was separate and was based on a belief that the players had come under so much pressure from journalists in the weeks before the championship that this was their only method of protesting and seeking a new way of dealing with the press.

The Rugby Union expressed its views on the matter to the squad at the next opportunity and said that a code of conduct would be drawn up for future matches so that players were fully aware of what would be expected of them in all areas. Cooke and Carling escaped further punishment but both were aware of the criticisms against them within the Rugby

Union committee. Pearey, as president, turned out to be a peace-maker. "I'm not keen on taking sanctions against anybody," he said.

England also had to continue with their playing commitments and I suggested in the *Sunday Express* that points were more important than payment and that all factors involving the amateur regulations and possible rewards had to be put aside to enable the players to concentrate on the championship. The ending of the relationship between WHJ Promotions and the England squad and the appointment of the Rugby Union's own marketing manager to look after their interests was eventual proof that the players had heeded advice to make winning their only objective.

Scotland were the next opponents, and their appearance at Twickenham would coincide with the formal opening of the £16m North Stand by the Princess Royal, who is patron of the Scottish Rugby Union. Heavy snowfalls before the game were dealt with by the ground staff ("Well done, boys in the snow" said the ground's electronic scoreboard when they completed the task) and England's unchanged side went out to erase the memory of 1990. "Nobody could wait for the chance to get at Scotland again," Brian Moore admitted.

Cooke had tightened England's preparations a little by holding a training session behind closed doors. Publicly he said that England would need to raise their game by 25 per cent over their Cardiff performance.

Scotland had only two changes from the previous game with England but one of them meant that Finlay Calder was missing. England imposed from the start, with Hodgkinson kicking goals after 15 and 17 minutes, and although Chalmers put Scotland level with two penalties, a third kick by Hodgkinson left England 9–6 ahead at half-time.

Ackford, Dooley and Richards took command of the line-out while Andrew's accurate kicking continually put England into pressure positions. One try was poor reward for all the English work but it did involve many facets of the team. In the 44th minute Ackford won a line-out. The ball was worked

238

to Winterbottom, who was only prevented from scoring by a crunching tackle from Jeffrey; but England again worked the ball out via Hodgkinson to Heslop who raced on for a try. Hodgkinson and Chalmers each kicked two more penalties, leaving England winners 21–12.

If England saw the season as a series of mental tests, two old scores were now out of the way. The Cardiff factor had been lain to rest and Scotland had been seen off. In prospect Ireland did not loom as anything like as difficult a test because England had a run of wins against the Irish and Ireland were trying to build a new team for the World Cup under a new coach, Ciaran Fitzgerald, the 1983 Lions captain.

Dublin provided a wet pitch and a ground jammed to capacity for Ireland's attempt to halt England's drive for the Triple Crown for the first time for eleven years. Ireland responded to all the fervour of the day by thundering into England, upsetting them at source and forcing them to turn and chase. England found the going hard in the wind and the dampness, and even Hodgkinson was affected, missing his first three penalty attempts. By half-time the score had progressed to 3–3, a penalty by Brian Smith from 55 yards for Ireland, one by Hodgkinson for England.

In the third minute of the second half Ireland gained a 7–3 lead when Simon Geoghegan, their right wing who was English-born and educated but whose father came from the West of Ireland, weaved past Underwood from close range for a try. This was the first time England had been seriously behind for almost a year and it needed only one more score by Ireland to take the game clear. However, they chose some wrong options and allowed England some breathing-space. Gradually the driving power of the England back row began to produce long periods of territorial advantage.

Ireland tackled prodigiously and escaped many times, but after Hodgkinson kicked a further penalty England attacked through Richards in the middle of the pitch and Andrew and Hodgkinson linked to put Underwood away. Ireland hurled defenders in Underwood's direction but he shifted his line of running a little and changed pace and was able to avoid the cover and score, his 26th try for his country in his 42nd game.

Another drive by Richards produced a try in injury time for Teague which Hodgkinson converted to take his personal score for the championship to 46 points, thus relieving Dusty Hare of his record which had stood since 1984. England won 16–7.

France beat Wales on the same day, and so for a second year running the championship brought together two unbeaten sides to decide it all – Grand Slam, title and the chance to spearhead Europe into the World Cup. Now England could go for it because in contrast to the two previous championships they were playing the final match at home – and without a Southern Hemisphere referee in charge: Les Peard of Wales had been appointed to referee the game.

There were two weeks to fill. For most of the players there were Courage League commitments on the intervening Saturday. Harlequins had a week off, which meant that Carling and the other Harlequins in the squad, seven in all, could do as they chose. Carling went shopping on the Saturday before the greatest game of his life. To all those who watched him closely he was cheerful and relaxed.

He also made sure he was busy. He opened a Nike Running on Air exhibition at the Science Museum in South Kensington and was one of the models along with Ackford, Hill and Moore when England's World Cup shirts – the first change of shirt since they began playing international matches – was launched at Twickenham. By the time England assembled on the Wednesday evening, however, their concentration was absolute.

There was only one burden on England before the France game, and that was the criticism which had accompanied their three wins. They were accused of being an unadventurous side playing safety-first rugby for the benefit of a goal-kicker – and their low try-count was produced in evidence to prove it.

The players knew of the criticism and occasionally responded to it; but they knew that in 1990 they had played some of the most glorious football which an England team had produced and they had ended up by being beaten in the decisive match against Scotland. Whatever anybody said a Grand Slam victory was not going to be taken away from them this time by playing outside the limits they had established. Such limits might have entailed a minimum of risk, but at least New Zealand, the most consistent side in the world, would have admired them for it. "Lots of people support us and say just finish the job and that is my gut feeling about what people want us to do," said Cooke.

France, led by Serge Blanco in his final match in the championship and winning his 85th cap, arrived making low-key noises. They had brought in some big, strong men to try to counter England in the line-out and loose, and they had all their feared runners on duty. The day before the game, as they trained at Windsor, France ambled through a few ploys, light-hearted and relaxed, a side ready for what lay in store for them but conscious that not many expected them to win. Maybe all this was deceptive nonsense by the French. Daniel Dubroca, who had succeeded the stern and unadventurous Jacques Fouroux as coach, had encouraged a broader approach to the game. As the thousands of spectators headed for Twickenham there was still a sense that England could just fall at the last hurdle.

Within 30 seconds of the match starting France were penalized for dragging down a maul and Hodgkinson kicked a penalty: England were on the way – or so it seemed. However, when in the tenth minute Hodgkinson missed a kick, France counter-attacked to score a try which defied belief. As Hodgkinson's kick towards the south-west upright dipped and fell, off target, the whole ground relaxed, waiting for a French drop-out. Instead France, via Blanco, pumped the ball hard along their in-goal area, heading east, before turning to run down the touchline.

As the ball was being carried on – by Blanco, Lafond and Sella – the sheer pace and audacity of the attack caught England unawares. Around half-way, Camberabero, the fly-half, who had the ball, chipped ahead and regathered. Looking inside him he could see the left wing Saint-André storming up the centre of the pitch and he cross-kicked into his path. The ball sat up for him perfectly. Saint-André seized it and easily outran the remnants of the England defence to score.

So the battle was joined. Andrew dropped a goal and Hodgkinson kicked a penalty to restore the England lead at 9–6, but Camberabero levelled the scores with a penalty after 26 minutes.

England's only try came next. Teague and Richards were in harness for a drive and Carling played the fly-half role to send Andrew away. Hodgkinson came into the line and his pass to Underwood gave the wing the chance to run clear of Lafond and score. Hodgkinson converted that and kicked a penalty so that at half-time England were ahead 18–9.

The lead was preserved throughout the second-half – but France won that half hands-down. Two tries, one by Camberabero after a chip through and a second by Mesnel after some inspiring play by Blanco, were balanced against Hodgkinson's lone penalty of the half. Mesnel's try put France within range at 19–21 with three minutes to play, and from being way out in front England were left with the agonies of those last moments, before the Grand Slam was irrevocably won and the fans swarmed on to the pitch and lifted any English player they could find to sweep him towards the dressing room.

Carling was one of those hoisted aloft. The boy who had begun playing at six and a half and won many a Grand Slam in his garden had now, on 16 March 1991, done so in reality. He was carried across the pitch at Twickenham like a cork and when they put him down he found that his boots had gone from his feet. As Carling was walking on air it hardly mattered.

CHAPTER 36

A Grand Slam means different things to different people but there was no doubt that it meant most to those who had been in the England squad the longest without anything to show for it. That is why, when England came off the pitch at Twickenham and on into the long night of celebration, it was easy to identify with the delight of Winterbottom, who started in 1982, with Teague and Hill and Underwood from 1984, with Dooley and Andrew from 1985. All these players must have wondered if they would spend long years in the England side and not earn a secure place in rugby history.

The three post-War Grand Slam teams which England have produced all bear the hallmark of constant selection which shows a belief in the players that translates into unity on the pitch. The 1980 team would always stress that they believed in the selections and the 1991 team would say exactly the same.

There is no magic formula for this. It is to do with identifying players who will blend in with a particular set of objectives. This is critical. Creation of confidence in what they are doing comes next, then the planning of targets. Fitness support is essential, as is mental preparation. Cooke left none of these areas neglected.

Judged on results over the years England are still a long way from fulfilment. For a nation with 1,900 clubs the international end of the sport has been nothing like as successful or consistent as it should have been. If some of the calls for a new structure had been acted upon instead of ignored in the sixties and seventies, maybe the levels of play which have been reached in the last few years would have been acquired earlier.

The signs now are promising. Since 1985, when the first World Cup was confirmed, the changes in rugby world-wide have been considerable, and England realize as much as anyone else that they must be part of the continuing search for better standards. The squad which played in the 1987 World Cup was a pioneer group. Despite intense work, England faltered against Wales. It is that sort of lapse and those that occurred against Wales in 1989 and Scotland in 1990 which the present England management are determined to eradicate.

The five nations' championship is a marvellous platform for the game. It is an ancient event in the long story of rugby, but remains compelling to audiences and players. However, on the evidence of 1987, the World Cup tests ability as never before – and will do so on a regular cycle. Come the 1991 World Cup no one can say this time that the English team has not had sufficient preparation.

It seems ludicrous that New Zealand, the holders, and England, the 1991 champions of Europe, should be drawn in the same group, but that is because the seedings were done long ago on the grounds of commercial expediency. Whether such criteria should continue will have to be studied in depth before the 1995 World Cup.

New Zealand's immense rugby heritage is the principal reason why they will be so difficult to dislodge in the World Cup. Rugby is New Zealand's national game and the country's greatest sporting expression. Great achievements in New Zealand rugby are passed on from generation to generation, giving the young the inspiration to equal or better the old. New Zealand's playing structure is well defined and players of promise are discovered quickly and led towards

245

the top. If they survive they are persisted with, and one of the pressures of playing for New Zealand is the knowledge that there might be half a dozen other players vying for your place.

The All Blacks recognize the value of a hard core of senior players which is why as the World Cup approaches there will be a minimum amount of change in their team. Gary Whetton took over the captaincy in 1990 in his 31st year. Yet this 6ft 6in. lock forward from Auckland had started with the All Blacks nine years earlier – three years ahead of his twin brother Alan, who is a flanker.

New Zealand's front row commands respect everywhere and is also unlikely to change, with Steve McDowell and Richard Loe propping Sean Fitzpatrick who won his place in 1986 when Andy Dalton, the nominated World Cup captain was injured: he has been there ever since.

Much as New Zealand's effort is dependent on the skill and staying-power of the forwards and the way they comprehensively cover the pitch, the scoring capabilities of their leading backs, Grant Fox and John Kirwan, are also vital. Fly-half Fox played throughout the first World Cup and is the most consistent kicker in international rugby. Kirwan, who has fully recovered from a ruptured Achilles tendon in 1989, is big and quick on the New Zealand right wing and is a devastating finisher.

Australia still have their high-scoring fly-half, Michael Lynagh, who passed the 500-point mark, a world record, after 43 appearances. Though Fox was the fastest player to 100 points, 200 points and 300 points, Lynagh may be difficult to overtake. Australia's other great scoring power is David Campese, who can play wing or full back. Campese has been playing for Australia since 1982 and has made seven overseas tours, captivating audiences with his running style.

Providing France can settle on the right combination of forwards, their back-play should be one of the most exciting ingredients of the World Cup. They play all their group matches and the prospective quarter-final in France. Blanco, whose impact in the first World Cup was considerable, says he doesn't intend to continue after the 1991 competition and will doubtless want to make his mark. He has plenty of runners in front of him to support – Philippe Sella and Franck Mesnel being the principal strikers.

Scotland, quarter-finalists last time before losing to New Zealand, could go at least one round further because the draw gives them the chance to play all the way through to the final without leaving Murrayfield. They have world-class players in captain David Sole at prop, half-backs Gary Armstrong and Craig Chalmers and Gavin Hastings at full-back, while Ian McGeechan's coaching will put Scotland at a peak.

Wales will have to hope that good things happen to them late in the day. They have taken a phenomenal and unprecedented battering since winning third place in 1987 and so badly need a few victories to put confidence back into the squad.

Coach Ron Waldron is charged with finding a pack of forwards to compete in a demanding World Cup group containing Australia, Argentina and Western Samoa, and may have only a handful of experienced men in his final squad – such as captain Paul Thorburn, wing Ieuan Evans and scrum-half Robert Jones.

Ireland made progress in 1991. Selection of young backs like Jim Staples, Simon Geoghegan, Dave Curtis and Rob Saunders gave the side fresh impetus and there is every chance that Ciaran Fitzgerald will mould a pack which will make an impact.

As for England, so much is possible. In Hodgkinson, whose 60 points in the 1991 championship was a record, they have a kicker who will frighten any opposition. In Underwood, who ended the championship with a record-equalling 43rd cap, they have a player with the finishing power to worry any defence. In Andrew and Hill they have half backs who can direct a game with their kicking as well

247

as set up one of the best midfield pairings in the world in Carling and Guscott.

Richards remains the most influential England forward, He is out on his own as a No. 8 and the World Cup campaign may hinge on his play and pack leadership.

The England forwards have had time to absorb the lessons of the Grand Slam before raising their concentration level once more for the World Cup – a competition in which seven of the Grand Slam side and ten of the match squad of 21 have had experience. For some of the senior forwards it will be their last chance – and there cannot be a greater motivation than that.

At the heart of all the playing activity stands William David Charles Carling, the soldier's son, a marksman with the power and pace to exploit a gap, an innovator, a flag-carrier, above all a player willing to do everything which he asks of others. When the Grand Slam was over Carling had played 24 times for England, 17 of them as captain. Thirteen victories have accompanied his captaincy. During the World Cup Carling is set to overhaul Bill Beaumont's record of 21 games as captain.

And after that? Carling was chosen by Cooke as captain and Cooke has backed him to the hilt, recognizing that Carling had to grow within the job and giving him the time and the space to do so. Cooke says that, depending on what criteria you use, Carling has it within him to become England's greatest captain. Whether he is success-ful or not – and thus far he has been successful – Carling is wise enough to realize that his future might depend on Cooke's continued support and his own interest in accept-ing all the tasks which he has dovetailed into the leader-ship.

Carling's office is almost on Piccadilly Circus in the heart of London, and that might be considered a perfect geographical setting to carry out the England captaincy the way he wants it. John Pullin, on his farm near the Severn Bridge, or Bill Beaumont, based in Lancashire, would not have been so instantly available for the activities in London and at Twickenham which Carling undertakes.

The Rugby Union may not always have been the pacesetters in the rapidly changing face of the game on a world basis; but the Rugby Union will not be left behind, and the physical growth of Twickenham, with massive new East and West stands due to be in position for the 21st century, has been at a pace which few of the early administrators could have contemplated.

Will Carling has been part of that pace, part of the scenario that has brought crowds and sponsorship and interest into English rugby as never before.

Acknowledgements

The author gratefully acknowledges the cooperation of the England rugby players and administrators, past and present; the inspiration of Jack Searle, the late Gerald Freeman, Reg Hayter, Tom Clark, Michael Heard and Peter Watson; the patience and accuracy of Ruth Mellor; the statistical brilliance of Terry Cooper; and the encouragement of Gerald Seymour.

Photographs . . . . pages 87–96

Allsport/David Cannon: 34, 36, 37
Alllsport/Russell Cheyne: 20
Bob Thomas Sport Photography: 6, 15, 25, 28
Colorsport: 3, 4, 7, 8, 9, 10, 12, 13, 17, 19, 21,
24, 26, 29, 30, 31, 32, 33, 35, 38, 39, 40
Express Newspapers: 11, 14, 16, 22, 23
Hulton-Deutsch Collection: 2
Mark Leech: 18
Popperfoto: 27
Syndication International Ltd: 1